Data Lakehouse in Action

Architecting a modern and scalable data analytics platform

Pradeep Menon

BIRMINGHAM—MUMBAI

Data Lakehouse in Action

Copyright © 2022 Packt Publishing

Publishing Product Manager: Sunith Shetty

Senior Editor: David Sugarman

Content Development Editor: Priyanka Soam

Technical Editor: Sonam Pandey

Copy Editor: Safis Editing

Project Coordinator: Aparna Ravikumar Nair

Proofreader: Safis Editing

Indexer: Sejal Dsilva

Production Designer: Joshua Misquitta

Marketing Coordinator: Abeer Riyaz Dawe

First published: March 2022

Production reference: 1070222

Published by Packt Publishing Ltd.

Livery Place

35 Livery Street

Birmingham

B3 2PB, UK.

ISBN 978-1-80181-593-2

www.packt.com

Many people have contributed to the creation of this book. From its inception to its publishing, my mentors, friends, colleagues, and family have constantly motivated, guided, and supported me. Unfortunately, there is not enough space to thank all of them. However, I will make five key mentions that were absolutely pivotal for creating this book.

Firstly, I want to thank my parents, who have supported me through the thick and thin of life. Their upbringing ensured that I was capable enough to undertake the Herculean task of writing a book.

Secondly, I want to thank my wife, Archana, and my daughter, Anaisha. They have constantly supported me while writing this book. They ensured that the boat was afloat as I burnt the midnight oil.

Thirdly, I want to thank my colleague and an accomplished architect, Debananda Ghosh. His technical knowledge, understanding of the complex dynamics of data, and honest feedback helped me make manifold improvements to this book's contents.

Fourthly, I want to thank the Packt Publishing team: Sunith Shetty, Priyanka Soam, Aishwarya Mohan, and David Sugarman. This team is an author's dream – open to ideas, dedicated, and diligent. I'm thankful for the fantastic support provided by the team that made the writing process an absolute pleasure.

And finally, I want to thank my best friend and beloved pet, Pablo (a beagle). Without him, I wouldn't have had a chance to complete any book. He has single-handedly made me disciplined in my approach to life. The dedication and focus required to complete a book are directly attributable to the discipline instilled in me by him.

Contributors

About the author

Pradeep Menon is a seasoned data analytics professional with more than 18 years of experience in data and AI.

Pradeep can balance business and technical aspects of any engagement and cross-pollinate complex concepts across many industries and scenarios.

Currently, Pradeep works as a data and AI strategist at Microsoft. In this role, he is responsible for driving big data and AI adoption for Microsoft's strategic customers across Asia.

Pradeep is also a distinguished speaker and blogger and has given numerous keynotes on cloud technologies, data, and AI.

About the reviewer

Debananda Ghosh is a senior specialist and global black belt (Cloud Analytics Asia) at Microsoft. He completed his bachelor's at Jadavpur University in B.Engineering, pursuing his postgraduate in data science and business analytics from McCombs School of Business at the University of Texas at Austin. He specializes in the fields of data and AI. His expertise includes data warehouses, DBA, data engineering, machine learning, data science product innovation, data and AI architecture and presales, and cloud analytics product sales. He has worked with customers in finance, manufacturing, utilities, telecoms, retail, e-commerce, and aviation. Currently working in the Microsoft Cloud Analytics product field, he helps industry partners achieve their digital transformation projects using advanced analytics and AI capabilities.

Table of Contents

Part 2: Data Lakehouse Component Deep Dive

3

Ingesting and Processing Data in a Data Lakehouse

4

Storing and Serving Data in a Data Lakehouse

Part 3: Implementing and Governing a Data Lakehouse

8
Implementing a Data Lakehouse on Microsoft Azure

9
Scaling the Data Lakehouse Architecture

Index
Other Books You May Enjoy

Preface

Digital transformation is a reality. All organizations, big or small, have to embrace this reality to be relevant in the future. Data is at the core of this, and data analytics is the catalyst for this transformation. Therefore, an agile, scalable, and robust data architecture for analytics is pivotal for forging data as a strategic asset.

However, very few organizations can successfully harness their data estate for analytics. Many of them grapple with obsolete enterprise data warehouse architectural patterns or have jumped onto the data lake bandwagon without a proper architectural framework. Also, the new trending term "Data Lakehouse" focuses on various vendors' product-centric views rather than an architectural paradigm. This book views the concept of Data Lakehouse through an architectural lens.

This book is a comprehensive framework for developing a modern data analytics architecture. While writing this book, I have focused on architectural constructs of a Data Lakehouse. The book covers different layers and components of architecture. It explores how these different layers interoperate to form a robust, scalable, and modular architecture that can be deployed on any platform.

By the end of this book, you will understand the need for a new data architecture pattern called Data Lakehouse, the details of the different layers and components of a Data Lakehouse architecture, and the methods required to deploy this architecture in a cloud computing platform and scale it to achieve the macro-patterns of Data Mesh and Hub-spoke.

Who this book is for

This book is for people who want to understand how to architect modern analytics. This book targets anyone who wants to become well-versed with modern data architecture patterns to enable large-scale analytics. It explains concepts in a non-technical and straightforward manner. The book's target audience includes data architects, big data engineers, data strategists and practitioners, data stewards, and cloud computing practitioners.

What this book covers

Chapter 1, Introducing the Evolution of Data Analytics Patterns, provides an overview of the evolution of the data architecture patterns for analytics.

Chapter 2, The Data Lakehouse Architecture Overview, provides an overview of the various components that form the Data Lakehouse architecture pattern.

Chapter 3, Ingesting and Processing Data in a Data Lakehouse, deep dives into the methods of ingesting and processing data in a batch and streaming data in a Data Lakehouse.

Chapter 4, Storing and Serving Data in a Data Lakehouse, discusses the types of datastores of a data lake and various methods of serving data from a Data Lakehouse.

Chapter 5, Deriving Insights from a Data Lakehouse, discusses the ways in which business intelligence, artificial intelligence, and data exploration can be carried out.

Chapter 6, Applying Data Governance in a Data Lakehouse, discusses how data can be governed, how to implement and maintain data quality, and how data needs to be cataloged.

Chapter 7, Applying Data Security in a Data Lakehouse, discusses various components used to secure the Data Lakehouse and ways to provide proper access to the right users.

Chapter 8, Implementing a Data Lakehouse on Microsoft Azure, focuses on implementing a Data Lakehouse on the Microsoft Azure cloud computing platform.

Chapter 9, Scaling the Data Lakehouse Architecture, discusses how Data Lakehouses can be scaled to realize the macro-architecture patterns of Data Mesh and Hub-spoke.

Download the color images

We also provide a PDF file that has color images of the screenshots/diagrams used in this book. You can download it here: https://static.packt-cdn.com/downloads/9781801815932_ColorImages.pdf.

Conventions used

Bold: Indicates a new term, an important word, or words that you see on screen. For instance, words in menus or dialog boxes appear in **bold**. Here is an example: "The two types of metadata that need to be cataloged include **Functional** and **Technical**."

Get in touch

Feedback from our readers is always welcome.

General feedback: If you have questions about any aspect of this book, mention the book title in the subject of your message and email us at customercare@packtpub.com.

Errata: Although we have taken every care to ensure the accuracy of our content, mistakes do happen. If you have found a mistake in this book, we would be grateful if you would report this to us. Please visit www.packtpub.com/support/errata, selecting your book, clicking on the Errata Submission Form link, and entering the details.

Piracy: If you come across any illegal copies of our works in any form on the internet, we would be grateful if you would provide us with the location address or website name. Please contact us at copyright@packt.com with a link to the material.

If you are interested in becoming an author: If there is a topic that you have expertise in and you are interested in either writing or contributing to a book, please visit authors.packtpub.com.

Share your thoughts

Once you've read *Data Lakehouse in Action*, we'd love to hear your thoughts! Scan the QR code below to go straight to the Amazon review page for this book and share your feedback.

https://packt.link/r/1-801-81593-3

Your review is important to us and the tech community and will help us make sure we're delivering excellent quality content.

PART 1: Architectural Patterns for Analytics

This section describes the evolution of data architecture patterns for analytics. It addresses the challenges posed by different architectural patterns and establishes a new paradigm, that is, the data lakehouse. An overview of the data lakehouse architecture is also provided, which includes coverage of the principles that govern the target architecture, the components that form the data lakehouse architecture, the rationale and need for those components, and the architectural principles adopted to make a data lake scalable and robust.

This section comprises the following chapters:

- *Chapter 1, Introducing the Evolution of Data Analytics Patterns*
- *Chapter 2, The Data Lakehouse Architecture Overview*

1
Introducing the Evolution of Data Analytics Patterns

Data analytics is an ever-changing field. A little history will help you appreciate the strides in this field and how data architectural patterns have evolved to fulfill the ever-changing need for analytics.

First, let's start with some definitions:

- What is **analytics**? Analytics is defined as any action that converts data into insights.
- What is **data architecture**? Data architecture is the structure that enables the storage, transformation, exploitation, and governance of data.

Analytics and the data architecture that enables analytics goes a long way. Let's now explore some of the patterns that have evolved over the last few decades.

This chapter explores the genesis of data growth and explains the need for a new paradigm in data architecture. This chapter starts by examining the predominant paradigm, the enterprise data warehouse, popular in the 1990s and 2000s. It explores the challenges associated with this paradigm and then covers the drivers that caused an explosion in data. It further examines the rise of a new paradigm, the data lake, and its challenges. Furthermore, this chapter ends by advocating the need for a new paradigm, the data lakehouse. It clarifies the key benefits delivered by a well-architected data lakehouse.

We'll cover all of this in the following topics:

- Discovering the enterprise data warehouse era
- Exploring the five factors of change
- Investigating the data lake era
- Introducing the data lakehouse paradigm

Discovering the enterprise data warehouse era

The **Enterprise Data Warehouse** (**EDW**) pattern, popularized by Ralph Kimball and Bill Inmon, was predominant in the 1990s and 2000s. The needs of this era were relatively straightforward (at least compared to the current context). The focus was predominantly on optimizing database structures to satisfy reporting requirements. Analytics was synonymous with reporting. Machine learning was a specialized field and was not ubiquitous in enterprises.

A typical EDW pattern is depicted in the following figure:

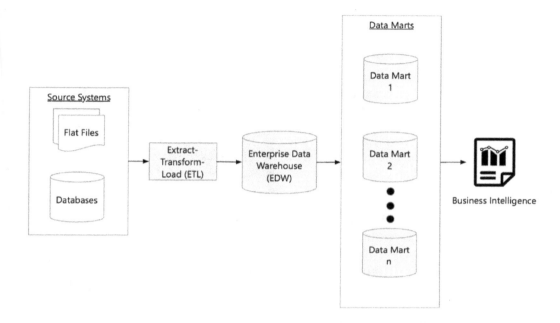

Figure 1.1 – A typical EDW pattern

As shown in *Figure 1.1*, the pattern entailed source systems composed of databases or flat-file structures. The data sources are predominantly structured, that is, rows and columns. A process called **Extract-Transform-Load** (**ETL**) first extracts the data from the source systems. Then, the process transforms the data into a shape and form that is conducive for analysis. Once the data is transformed, it is loaded into an EDW. From there, the subsets of data are then populated to downstream data marts. Data marts can be conceived of as *mini data warehouses* that cater to the business requirements of a specific department.

As you can imagine, this pattern primarily was focused on the following:

- Creating a data structure that is optimized for storage and modeled for reporting
- Focusing on the reporting requirements of the business
- Harnessing the structured data into actionable insights

Every coin has two sides. The EDW pattern is not an exception. It has its pros and it has its cons. This pattern has survived the test of time. It was widespread and well adopted because of the following key advantages:

- Since most of the analytical requirements were related to reporting, this pattern effectively addressed many organizations' reporting requirements.

- Large enterprise data models were able to structure an organization's data into logical and physical models. This pattern gave a structure to manage the organization's data in a modular and efficient manner.

- Since this pattern catered only to structured data, the technology required to harness structured data was evolved and readily available. **Relational Database Management Systems (RDBMSes)** evolved and were juxtaposed appropriately to harness its features for reporting.

However, it also had its own set of challenges that surfaced as the data volumes grew and new data formats started emerging. A few challenges associated with the EDW pattern are as follows:

- This pattern was not as agile as the changing business requirements wanted it to be. Any change in the reporting requirement had to go through a long-winded process of data model changes, ETL code changes, and respective changes to the reporting system. Often, the ETL process was a specialized skill and became a bottleneck for reducing data to insight turnover time. The nature of analytics is unique. The more you see the output, the more you demand. Many EDW projects were deemed a failure. The failure was not from a technical perspective, but from a business perspective. Operationally, the design changes required to cater to these fast-evolving requirements were too difficult to handle.

- As the data volumes grew, this pattern proved too cost prohibitive. Massive parallel-processing database technologies started evolving that specialized in data warehouse workloads. The cost of maintaining these databases was prohibitive as well. It involved expensive software prices, frequent hardware refreshes, and a substantial staffing cost. The return on investment was no longer justifiable.

- As the format of data started evolving, the challenges associated with the EDW became more evident. Database technologies were developed to cater to semi-structured data (**JSON**). However, the fundamental concept was still RDBMS-based. The underlying technology was not able to effectively cater to these new types of data. There was more value in analyzing data that was not structured. The sheer variety of data was too complex for EDWs to handle.

- The EDW was focused predominantly on **Business Intelligence** (**BI**). It facilitated the creation of scheduled reports, ad hoc data analysis, and self-service BI. Although it catered to most of the personas who performed analysis, it was not conducive to AI/ML use cases. The data in the EDW was already cleansed and structured with a razor-sharp focus on reporting. This left little room for a data scientist (statistical modelers at that time) to explore data and create a new hypothesis. In short, the EDW was primarily focused on BI.

While the EDW pattern was becoming mainstream, a perfect storm was flourishing that changed the landscape. The following section will focus on five different factors that came together to change the data architecture pattern for good.

Exploring the five factors of change

The year 2007 changed the world as we know it; the day Steve Jobs took the stage and announced the iPhone launch was a turning point in the age of data. That day brewed the perfect "data" storm.

A perfect storm is a meteorological event that occurs as a result of a rare combination of factors. In the world of data evolution, such a perfect storm occurred in the last decade, one that has catapulted data as a strategic enterprise asset. Five ingredients caused the perfect "data" storm.

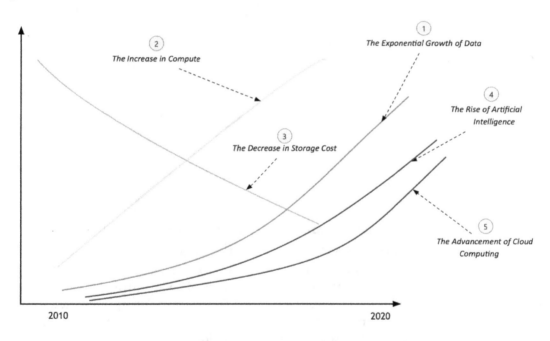

Figure 1.2 – Ingredients of the perfect "data" storm

As depicted in *Figure 1.2*, there were five factors to the perfect storm. An exponential growth of data and an increase in computing power were the first two factors. These two factors coincided with a decrease in storage cost. The rise of AI and the advancement of cloud computing coalesced at the same time to form the perfect storm.

These factors developed independently and converged together, changing and shaping industries. Let's look into each of these factors briefly.

The exponential growth of data

The exponential growth of data is the first ingredient of the perfect storm.

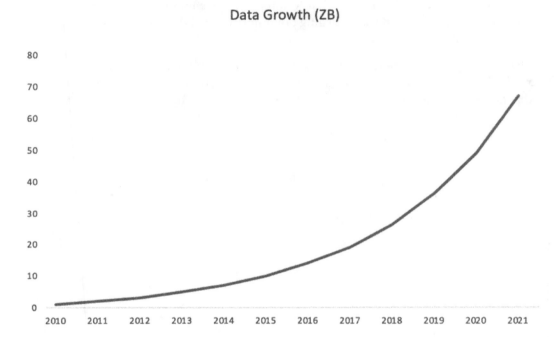

Figure 1.3 – Estimated data growth between 2010 and 2020

According to the **International Data Corporation** (**IDC**), by 2025, the total data volumes generated will reach around 163 ZB (zettabytes), that is, a trillion gigabytes. In 2010, that number was approximately 0.5 ZB. This exponential growth of data is attributed to a vast improvement in internet technologies that have fueled the growth of many industries. The telecommunications industry was the major industry that was transformed. This, in turn, transformed many other industries. Data became ubiquitous and every business craved more data bandwidth. Social media platforms started to be used as well. The likes of Facebook, Twitter, and Instagram flooded the internet space with more data. Streaming services and e-commerce also generated tons of data. This generated data was used to forge and influence consumer behaviors. Last, but not least, the technological leaps in the **Internet of Things** (**IoT**) space generated loads of data.

The traditional EDW pattern was not able to cope with this growth in data. They were designed for structured data. Big data had changed the definition of usable data. The data now was big (volume); some of them were continuously flowing (velocity), generated in different shapes and forms (variety), and from a plethora of sources with noise (veracity).

The increase in compute

The exponential increase in computing power is the second ingredient of the perfect storm.

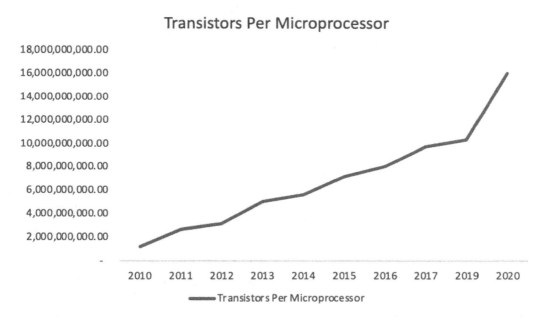

Figure 1.4 – Estimated growth in transistors per microprocessors between 2010 and 2020

Moore's law is the prediction made by American engineer Gordon Moore in 1965 that the number of transistors per silicon chip doubles every year. This law has been faithful to its forecast so far. In 2010, the number of transistors in a microprocessor was around 2 billion. In 2020, that number stood at 54 billion. This exponential increase in computing power dovetails with the rise of cloud computing technologies that provide limitless compute at an affordable price point.

The increase in computing power at a reasonable price point provided a much-needed impetus for big data. Organizations can now procure more and more compute at a much lower price point. The compute available in cloud computing can now be used to process and analyze data on demand.

The decrease in storage cost

The rapid decrease in storage cost is the third ingredient of the perfect storm.

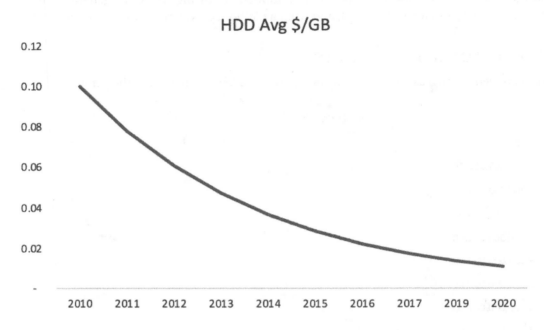

Figure 1.5 – The estimated decrease in storage cost between 2010 and 2020

The cost of storage has also exponentially decreased. In 2010, the average cost of storing a GB of data in a **Hard Disk Drive** (**HDD**) was around $0.1. That number has reduced to approximately $0.01 in 10 years. In the traditional EDW pattern, organizations had to be picky about which data they had to store for analysis and which data could be discarded. Holding data was an expensive proposition. However, the exponential decrease in storage cost meant that all data could now be stored at a fraction of the previous cost. There was now no need to pick and choose what should be stored and what should be discarded. Data in whatever shape or form could now be kept at a fraction of price. The mantra of *store first and analyze later* could now be implemented.

The rise of artificial intelligence

Artificial Intelligence (**AI**) systems are not new to the world. In fact, their genesis goes back to the 1950s, when statistical models were used to estimate values of data points based on past data. This field was out of focus for an extended period, as the computing power and large corpus of data required to run these models were not available.

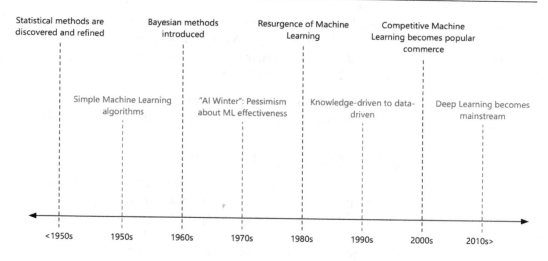

Figure 1.6 – Timeline of the evolution of AI

However, after a long hibernation, AI technologies saw a resurgence in the early 2010s. This resurgence was partly due to the abundance of powerful computing resources and the equal availability of data. AI models now could be trained faster, and the results were stunningly accurate.

The factor of reduced storage cost and more available computing resources was a boon for AI. More and more complex models could now be trained.

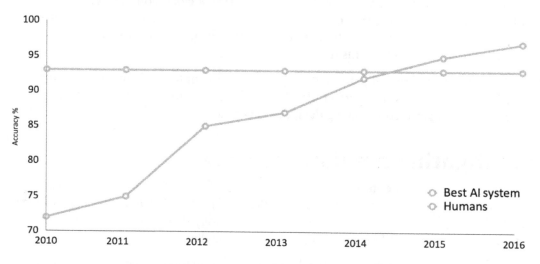

Figure 1.7 – Accuracy of AI systems in matching humans for image recognition

This was especially true for deep learning algorithms. For instance, a deep learning technique called **Convoluted Neural Networks (CNNs)** has become very popular for detecting images. Over a period, deeper and deeper neural networks were created. Now, AI systems have surpassed human beings in detecting objects.

As AI systems became more accurate, they gained in popularity. This fueled cyclic behavior, and more and more businesses were employing AI in their digital transformation agenda.

The advancement of cloud computing

The fifth ingredient for the perfect "data" storm is the rise of cloud computing. Cloud computing is the on-demand availability of computing and storage resources. The typical public cloud service providers include big technology companies such as Amazon (AWS), Microsoft (Azure), and Google (GCP). Cloud computing eliminates the need to host large servers for computing and storage on the organization's data center. Depending on the service subscribed to in the cloud, organizations can also reduce their dependencies on software and hardware maintenance. Cloud provides a plethora of on-demand services at a very economical price point. The cloud computing landscape has constantly been rising since 2010. Worldwide spending on public clouds started at around $77 billion in 2010 and has reached around $441 billion in 2020. Cloud computing also enabled the rise of the **Digitally Native Business (DNB)**. It propelled the rise of organizations such as Uber, Deliveroo, TikTok, and Instagram, to name a few.

Cloud computing has been a boon for data. With the rise of cloud computing, data can now be stored at a fraction of the cost. The comparatively limitless compute power that the cloud provides translates into the ability to rapidly transform data. Cloud computing also provides innovative data platforms that can be utilized at a click of a button.

These five ingredients crossed paths at an opportune moment to challenge the existing data architecture patterns. The perfect "data" storm facilitated the rise of a new data architecture paradigm focused on big data, **the data lake**.

Investigating the data lake era

The genesis of the data lake starts in 2004. In 2004, Google researchers Jeffery Dean and Sanjay Ghemawat published a paper titled *MapReduce: Simplified Data Processing on Large Clusters*. This paper laid the foundation of a new technology that evolved into Hadoop, whose original authors are Doug Cutting and Mike Cafarella.

Hadoop was later incorporated into Apache Software Foundation, a decentralized open source community of developers. Hadoop has been one of the top open source projects within the Apache ecosystem.

Hadoop was based on a simple concept – divide and conquer. The idea entailed three steps:

1. Distribute data into multiple files and distribute them across the various nodes in a cluster.

2. Use compute nodes to process the data locally in the nodes of each cluster.

3. Use an orchestrator that communicates with each node and aggregates data for the final output.

Over the years, this concept gained traction, and a new kind of paradigm emerged for analytics. This architecture paradigm is the data lake paradigm. A typical data lake pattern can be depicted in the following figure:

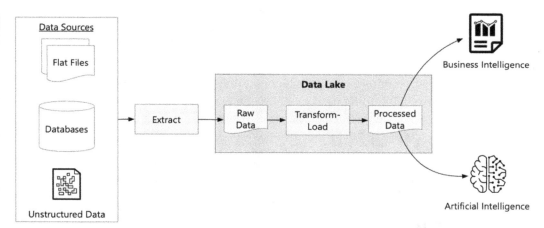

Figure 1.8 – A typical data lake pattern

This pattern addressed the challenges prevalent in the EDW pattern. The advantages that the data lake architecture pattern can offer are evident. The key advantages are as follows:

*   The data lake caters to both structured and unstructured data. The Hadoop ecosystem was primarily developed to store and process data formats such as JSON, text, and images. The EDW pattern was not designed to store or analyze these data types.

*   The data lake pattern can process large volumes of data at a relatively cheaper cost. The volumes of data that data lakes can store and process are in the order of high **Terabytes (TBs)** or **Petabytes (PB)**. The EDW pattern found these large volumes of data challenging to store and process efficiently.

*   Data lakes can better address fast-changing business requirements. The evolving AI technologies can leverage data lakes better.

This pattern is widely adopted as it is the need of the hour. However, it has its own challenges. A few challenges associated with this pattern are as follows:

- It is easy for a data lake to become a data swamp. Data lakes take in data, any form of data, and store it in its raw form. The philosophy is to ingest data first and then figure out what to do with it. This causes easy slippage of governance, and it becomes challenging to govern the data lake. With no proper data governance, data starts to mushroom all over the place in a data lake, and soon it becomes a data swamp.

- Data lakes also have challenges with the rapid evolution of technology. The data lake paradigm mainly relies on open source software. Open source software evolves rapidly into behemoths that can become too difficult to manage. The software is predominantly community-driven, and it doesn't have proper enterprise support. This causes a lot of maintenance overhead and implementation complexities. Many features that are demanded by enterprises are missing from open source software, for example, a robust security framework.

- Data lakes focus a lot more on AI enablement than BI. It was natural that the open source software evolution focused more on enabling AI. AI was having its own journey and was riding the wave, cresting together with Hadoop. BI was seen as retro, as it was already mature in its life cycle.

Soon, it became evident that the data lake pattern alone wouldn't be sustainable in the long run. There was a need for a new paradigm that fuses these two patterns.

Introducing the data lakehouse paradigm

In 2006, Clive Humbly, a British mathematician, coined the now-famous phrase, *"Data is the new oil."* It was akin to peering through a crystal ball and peeking into the future. Data is the lifeblood of organizations. The competitive advantage is defined by how an organization uses data. Data management is paramount in this age of digital transformation. More and more organizations are embracing digital transformation programs, and data is at the core of these transformations.

As discussed earlier, the paradigms of the EDW and data lakes were opportune for their times. They had their benefits and their challenges. A new paradigm needed to emerge that was *disciplined at its core and flexible at its edges*.

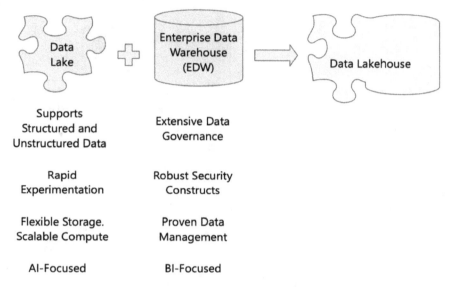

Figure 1.9 – Data lakehouse paradigm

The new data architectural paradigm is called the data lakehouse. It strives to combine the advantages of both the data lake and the EDW paradigms while minimizing their challenges.

An adequately architected data lakehouse delivers four key benefits.

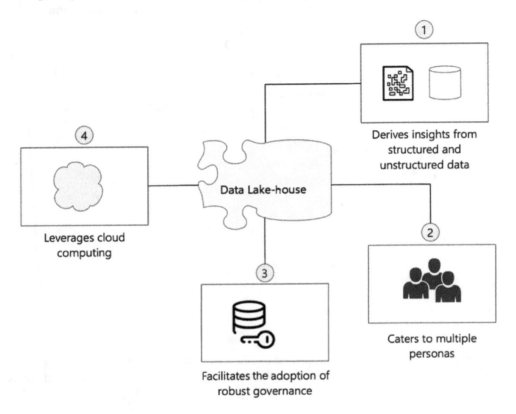

Figure 1.10 – Benefits of the data lakehouse

1. *It derives insights from both structured and unstructured data*: The data lakehouse architecture should be able to store, transform, and integrate structured and unstructured data. It should be able to fuse them together and enable the extraction of valuable insights from the data.

2. *It caters to different personas of the organizations*: Data is a dish with different tastes for different personas. The data lakehouse should be able to cater to the needs of these personas. The data lakehouse caters to a range of organizational personas and fulfills their requirements for insights. A data scientist should get their playground for testing their hypothesis. An analyst should be able to analyze data using their tools of choice, and business users should be able to get their reports accurately and on time. It democratizes data for analytics.

3. *It facilitates the adoption of a robust governance framework*: The primary challenge with the data lake architecture pattern was the lack of a strong governance framework. It was easy for a data lake to become a data swamp. In contrast, an EDW architecture was stymied by too much governance for too little content. The data lakehouse architecture strives to hit the governance balance. It seeks to achieve the proper governance for the correct data type with access to the right stakeholder.

4. *It leverages cloud computing*: Data lakehouse architecture needs to be agile and innovative. The pattern needs to adapt to the changing organizational requirements and reduce the data to insight turnover time. To achieve this agility, it is imperative to adopt cloud computing technology. The cloud computing platforms offer the innovativeness required. It provides the appropriate technology stack with scalability and flexibility, and fulfills the demands of a modern data analytics platform.

The data lakehouse paradigm addresses the challenges faced by the EDW and the data lake paradigm. Yet, it does have its own set of challenges that needs to be managed. A few of those challenges are as follows:

- *Architectural complexity*: Given that the data lakehouse pattern amalgamates the EDW and the data lake pattern, it is inevitable that it will have its fair share of architectural complexity. The complexity manifests in the form of multiple components required to fruition the pattern. Architectural patterns are quid pro quo; it is vital to carefully trade off architectural complexity with the potential business benefit. The data lakehouse architecture needs to tread that path carefully.

- *Required holistic data governance*: The challenges pertinent to the data lake paradigm do not magically go away with the data lakehouse paradigm. The biggest challenge of a data lake was that it was prone to becoming a data swamp. As the data lakehouse grows in its scope and complexity, the lack of a holistic governance framework is a sure-shot way of creating a swamp out of a data lakehouse.

- *Balancing flexibility with discipline*: The data lakehouse paradigm strives to be flexible and to adapt to changing business requirements with agility. The ethos under which it operates is to have discipline at the core and flexibility at the edges. Achieving this objective is a careful balancing act that clearly defines the limits of flexibility and the strictness of discipline. The data lakehouse stewards play an essential role in ensuring this balance.

Let's recap what we've discussed in this chapter.

Summary

This chapter was about the genesis of a new paradigm. It is important to have a view of the genesis so that we understand the shortcomings of the predecessors and how new frameworks can evolve to address these shortcomings. Understanding the drivers that caused this evolution is also important. Developments in other fields of technology such as storage, cloud computing, and AI have had a ripple effect on data architecture. In this chapter, we started out by exploring the EDW architecture pattern that was predominant for a long time. Then, we explored the factors that created the perfect "data" storm. Subsequently, the chapter delved into the data lake architecture pattern. The need for a new architectural paradigm, the data lakehouse, was then discussed. The chapter concluded by highlighting the critical benefits of the new architectural paradigm.

The next chapter aims to zoom in on the components of the data lakehouse architecture.

Further reading

- *The Data Warehouse Lifecycle Toolkit*: www.amazon.sg/Data-Warehouse-Lifecycle-Toolkit/dp/0470149779

- *Building the Data Warehouse*: https://www.amazon.com/Building-Data-Warehouse-W-Inmon/dp/0764599445

- *Simplified Data Processing on Large Clusters*: https://static.googleusercontent.com/media/research.google.com/en//archive/mapreduce-osdi04.pdf

- *Data Age 2025: The Evolution of Data to Life-Critical, David Reinsel, John Gantz, and John Rydning* (April 2017): www.import.io/wp-content/uploads/2017/04/Seagate-WP-DataAge2025-March-2017.pdf

- *Hard Disk Drive Quarterly Results and Projections, Tom Coughlin* (August 12, 2020): www.forbes.com/sites/tomcoughlin/2020/08/12/hard-disk-drive-quarterly-results-and-projections/?sh=2fe9a3412c5a

- *The Cloud Cover Spread Far and Beyond*: https://www.cxotoday.com/news-analysis/2010-2019-the-cloud-cover-spread-far-and-beyond/

2
The Data Lakehouse Architecture Overview

A well-thought-out architecture is the cornerstone of any robust **information technology** (**IT**) system, and a data lakehouse is no exception. The last chapter elucidated the need for a modern data analytics platform. The chapter also discussed the evolution of the data lakehouse. This chapter will focus on the critical elements of a data lakehouse.

The chapter will begin by describing the system context of a data lakehouse. Then, it will investigate the actors and systems that interact with a data lakehouse.

We will then discuss the logical architecture of a data lakehouse that consists of seven layers. The chapter will then deep-dive into various components of a data lakehouse architecture and elaborate on each element. The last section of this chapter will focus on five sacrosanct architecture principles that provide a framework for implementing a data lakehouse.

To summarize, the chapter covers the following topics:

- Developing a system context for a data lakehouse
- Developing a logical data lakehouse architecture
- Developing architecture principles

Developing a system context for a data lakehouse

A system context diagram shows different entities that interact with a system. In the following case, the system is a data lakehouse:

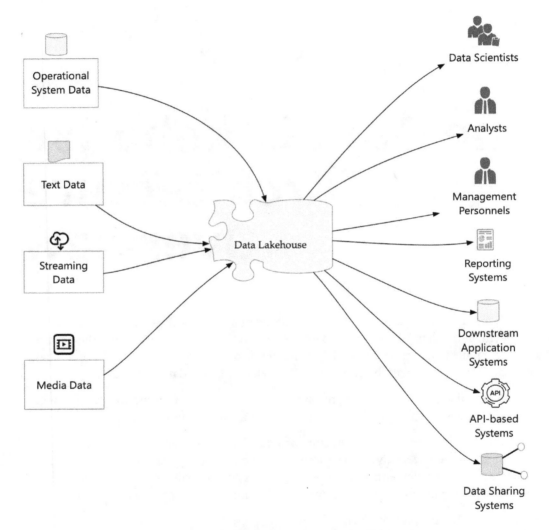

Figure 2.1 – Data lakehouse system context diagram

The preceding diagram shows key entities (systems or actors) that interact with the data lakehouse. The interaction with the data lakehouse has two parts, as outlined here:

- **Data providers**: Systems or actors that provide data to the data lakehouse
- **Data consumers**: Systems or actors that consume data from the data lakehouse

Let's examine these entities in detail.

Data providers

Data providers are any system or actor that ingests data into the data lakehouse. Any system that generates data is a potential data provider. A few typical data providers are listed here:

- **Operational systems**: Any system that generates data is a potential data provider. Typically, **online transaction processing (OLTP)** systems generate and store transactional data. The data in such systems is stored in relational databases in a highly normalized manner. As the data is highly normalized, the design is optimized for capturing and updating transactions effectively. Such systems are not suitable for analysis. OLTP systems are widespread in all organizations and form the majority of structured data stores. However, not all operational data is relational. The other form of operational data stores includes **Not-Only SQL (NoSQL)** databases. Data in a NoSQL database is not tabular. It is designed to store data in a flexible schema, and its structure can quickly adapt based on the input data type. Such databases store data in various formats, including key-value pairs, graphs, and **JavaScript Object Notation (JSON)**.

- **Text data**: When it comes to unstructured data/documents, text data is the most predominant type of unstructured data. This kind of data includes documents and plain texts such as handwritten notes. With **natural language processing (NLP)**, an established branch of **artificial intelligence (AI)**, we can extract a treasure trove of insights out of text data. AI algorithms are becoming more and more sophisticated in their ability to analyze texts.

- **Streaming data**: Data is found not just at rest. There is a category of data that is in motion. Streaming data implies data that is constantly transmitted from a system in a fixed time. Streaming data includes telemetry data emanated from any **internet of things** (IoT) device, constant feeds from social media platforms (Twitter, Facebook (Meta), YouTube, clickstream, gaming, and so on), continuous data flowing from financial trading platforms, and geospatial services that transmit location information. If analyzed in real time, this kind of data fulfills a gamut of use cases such as **complex event processing** (CEP), sentiment analysis, keyword detection, and so on.

- **Media data**: Media data includes various data structures associated with speech, video, and images. We can use **audio data** to fulfill use cases such as voice recognition, speech-to-text translation, and real-time voice translation. Media data also includes **videos and pictures** that we can use to perform an extensive range of use cases. AI algorithms such as **convolutional neural networks** (CNN) have advanced to the point that they are better suited for identifying objects in an image than humans. With a large corpus of video and image data, AI technologies are being used to fulfill advanced use cases ranging from object detection to self-driving cars.

We have seen typical data providers and a slice of use cases that these types of data can fulfill. Now, let's focus on who are the stakeholders that will use the data from a data lakehouse.

The following table summarizes the key data providers, the type of data, and the typical use cases that are fulfilled:

Data provider	Data type	Typical use case
Operational system data	Structured—relational	Reporting; data analysis; data for AI
Text data	Unstructured—documents; plain texts	NLP; text translation
Streaming data	Semi-structured—JSON	CEP; SA
Media data	Unstructured—images; video; audio files	Audio analytics; video analytics; object recognition; optical character recognition (OCR)

Figure 2.2 – Typical data providers and use cases

Next, let's look at who is going to use the data.

Data consumers

Once the data is ingested into the data lakehouse, various stakeholders will use it in its raw or transformed form. These stakeholders will **extract** data from the data lakehouse for a specific purpose. Each of these consumers has a personal motivation to use the data lakehouse. A well-architected data lakehouse should be able to cater to the requirements of each of these stakeholders. Let's look at some typical people and systems that consume data from a data lakehouse, as follows:

- **Data scientists**: The first type of people we see using a data lakehouse are data scientists, who extract data from the data lakehouse to test the various hypotheses they might want to prove or disprove. Data scientists work on all kinds of data: structured, unstructured, raw, and processed. The data lakehouse needs to be able to ensure that the data is easily identifiable for a specific purpose of use, the user must be proficient in many programming languages and technologies, including Python, R, and **Structured Query Language** (**SQL**), and the architecture needs to provide the right platform for this user to create and test their models.

- **Analysts**: The second type of people who use a data lakehouse are analysts. They are primarily business-driven and seek answers to business questions, and are proficient in reporting tools or SQL-based languages. They mainly work on processed data, and their day-to-day jobs include performing business analysis. They accomplish this task by querying, aggregating, and slicing/dicing data, mostly cleaned and processed. The data lakehouse should cater to such users and provide them with a platform to perform effective and seamless data analysis.

- **Management personnel**: The third type of people who are heavy users of data lakehouses are management personnel who need periodic reports for business decision-making. They delve into processed data that is aggregated and specifically focused on a business requirement. They may be semi tech-savvy and may need a playground to create their reports or analysis using **business intelligence** (**BI**) tools. These people generally extract their reports through a reporting system.

- **Reporting systems**: The other critical consumers of a data lakehouse are the reporting systems. Reporting systems indirectly cater to people who want to subscribe to scheduled, ad hoc, or self-service reports. In addition, there may be other types of reporting systems that are meant for regulatory reporting. These systems extract data from the data lakehouse periodically and then store the reports for delivery.

- **Downstream application systems**: As data is ingested into the data lakehouse from upstream applications, downstream applications also consume processed information. These applications may be an OLTP system or another data warehouse or data lake with a different mandate from an **enterprise data lakehouse** (EDL). Typically, data for downstream consumption will be either pulled from the data lakehouse periodically or pushed to a destination using a feasible mechanism.

- **Application programming interface (API)-based systems**: A data lakehouse also needs to have the ability to expose the data in the form of an API. A data lakehouse processes all kinds of data, and it needs to be served to multiple internal and external systems. While a tightly coupled delivery mechanism may work for select consumers, API-based data consumption is a scalable and practical option. In addition, an API-based system can also expose data consumed by external stakeholders who are not part of the organization.

- **Data sharing systems**: Data sharing systems represent a new type of data-consuming mechanism. This kind of mechanism is used when the data is consumed or shared as part of a data marketplace. The data-sharing mechanism is also employed when specific terms for data usage need to be agreed upon before subscribing to its consumption.

The following table summarizes the key motivation and typical requirements of data consumers:

Data consumer	Motivation	Typical use cases
Data scientists	To develop AI models	AI; machine learning (ML)
Analysts	To perform data analysis	Data analysis
Management personnel	To create operational or management reports	Scheduled reports; self-service BI
Reporting systems	To facilitate report creation	Report creation
Downstream application systems	To streamline operations using processed data	Utilization of processed data for business operations
API-based systems	To share data on a real-time basis	Sharing data to external or internal parties in a decoupled manner
Data sharing systems	To share data in a streamlined and controlled manner	Data marketplace monitored and controlled data sharing

Figure 2.3 – Typical data consumers and use cases

So, now we know who might be using our lakehouse, let's start thinking about how to build it.

Developing a logical data lakehouse architecture

We have discussed a data lakehouse system context. Let's now get into developing a logical data lakehouse architecture. A logical architecture focuses on components that integrate to satisfy specific **functional requirements (FRs)** and **non-functional requirements (NFRs)**. It is abstracted to a level that is technology-agnostic and focuses on component functionality. A logical architecture focuses on two kinds of requirements, as follows:

- An **FR** is a requirement that fulfills a specific business or domain-driven behavior. These kinds of requirements are driven by the tasks and the needs of a particular business function.

- An **NFR** is a requirement that specifies criteria that need to be fulfilled for the system to be helpful in that specific context. For example, a typical NFR includes the time a particular query is expected to complete, a requirement for data encryption, and so on.

A **well-architected system** ensures that it is architected to fulfill the NFR without too much trade-off. The following diagram depicts a logical architecture of a data lakehouse:

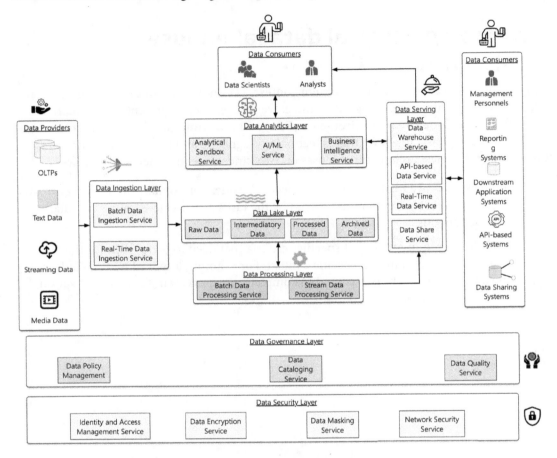

Figure 2.4 – A logical data lakehouse architecture

As depicted in the preceding diagram, a data lakehouse architecture has seven layers that weave together to form a well-architected data lakehouse. Let's now investigate each of these layers in detail.

Data ingestion layer

The first layer to detail is the data ingestion layer. This layer is the integration point between the external data providers to the data lakehouse. There are two types of data ingestion services, as illustrated in the following diagram:

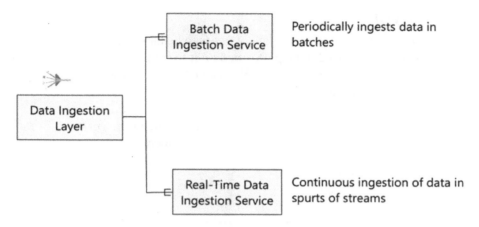

Figure 2.5 – Types of data ingestion services

These are explained in more detail here:

- **Batch Data Ingestion Service**: The batch ingestion implies that data is periodically ingested into the data lakehouse. The frequency of ingestion may range from a few minutes to days. The periodic frequency would depend on many factors, including the NFRs, the ability of data sources to generate data, and the ability of data sources to push data or allow the service to pull data. Typical operational systems require data to be pushed or pulled into the data lakehouse. A critical consideration to have while ingesting data in batches is the availability of the source system for data ingestion and the size of the batch data ingested. Both these factors will have an impact on how the data is ingested into the data lakehouse.

- **Real-Time Data Ingestion Service**: The real-time data ingestion service enables data to be pulled into the data lakehouse as it is generated. Real-time data is a constant stream of data, therefore the data of interest must be identified and pulled into the data lakehouse for storage or real-time processing. Real-time ingestion typically consists of a queuing service such as Kafka that would enable the real-time streams to be grouped and stored temporarily as queues for ingestion. Streaming services are also used to continuously capture data changes in databases through **change data capture** (**CDC**). Considerations related to the throughput of the streaming data and the requirements related to latencies become important while ingesting streaming data.

Data lake layer

Once the data ingestion layer ingests the data, it needs to be landed into storage, and various transformations need to be performed on it to transform the data for consumption. Finally, the data is anchored in the data lake. You can see a visual representation of this layer here:

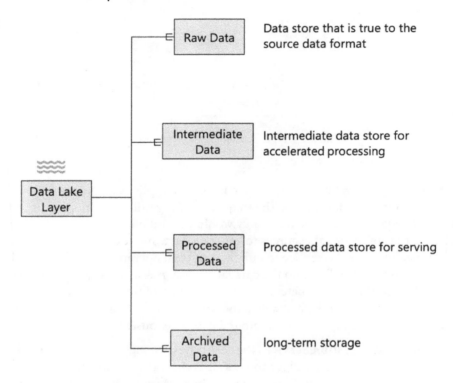

Figure 2.6 – Types of data stores in the data lake layer

The data lake layer has four significant categories of storage, as outlined here:

- **Raw Data**: Raw data storage is the area where the data lands from the data provider. As the name suggests, the data is stored in the raw data store in its natural form. Thus, the data is true to its source format, structure, and content. The raw data store also enables you to decouple the data generators with the data lakehouse.

- **Intermediate Data**: As the data traverses through the data lakehouse and is transformed, intermediary datasets are created. These intermediate datasets can be transient or persistent. These datasets can be stored in the data lake layer and can accelerate data processing. Intermediate data also makes the data processing pipeline immune to full restarts.

- **Processed Data**: Once the data is transformed, we can store the resultant dataset in the data lake. This dataset can then be used for serving or for analytics purposes. The processed data is suited for downstream consumption. However, the processed data in the data lake layer offers a relatively cheaper cost for storage. It also enables data scientists and analysts to use the processed data for experimentation or analysis without the overhead to the serving layer.

- **Archived Data**: The data that is consumed for insights is generally **hot**. Hot data implies that the storage technology used to store data ensures a better throughput and accessibility. However, not all data needs to be hot. Data that is not used for analytics but is required to be stored can be moved into cheaper storage technology. This kind of data is called archived data.

Data processing layer

The data needs to be transformed or processed for it to be consumed for insights. Data processing services perform the job of converting data that is ingested into a form that we can serve to the stakeholders. You can see a visual representation of this layer here:

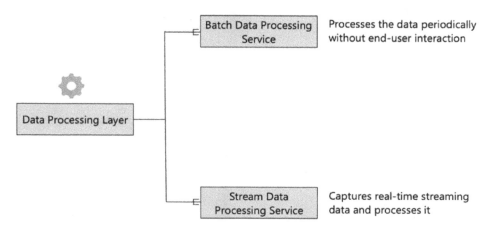

Figure 2.7 – Types of data processing services

There are two types of data processing services, as outlined here:

- **Batch Data Processing Service**: Batch data processing processes the data periodically without end-user interaction. The data is first landed in the raw data zone. Once the data lands in the raw data zone, the batch processing service picks up the raw data and performs the required transformation. Batch data processing services need to be on-demand and can be scaled as per your needs.

- **Stream Data Processing Service**: The other kind of processing is stream data processing. This captures real-time streaming data and processes it without needing the data to be landed or stored on a disk. All the stream processing happens in the memory, and data is transformed near real-time. A typical stream data processing service also has a **message queuing** layer that intermittently captures the data streams and queues them for further processing. When the data stream is ingested and processed, the raw data is sent to the data lake store for storage as one path. Another path does the real-time processing and sends the output for downstream consumption. Finally, the transformed data is also pushed into the data lake layer for persistent storage.

Next, let's cover the data serving layer.

Data serving layer

Once the data is processed, it needs to be served for downstream consumption. The information is made available to various stakeholders, and each of them has requirements tailored to their needs. You can see the services that make up this layer in the following diagram:

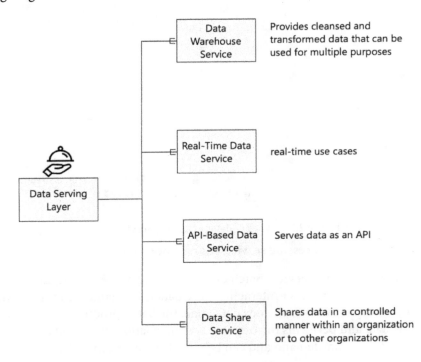

Figure 2.8 – Types of data-serving services

In general, there are four types of data-serving services, outlined as follows:

- **Data Warehouse Service**: The first type of data-serving service is the data warehouse service. A data warehouse service provides cleansed and transformed data that can be used for multiple purposes. First, it serves as a layer for reporting and BI. Second, it is a platform to query data for business or data analysis. Third, it serves as a repository to store historical data that needs to be online and available. Finally, it also acts as a source of transformed data for other downstream data marts that may cater to specific departmental requirements.

- **Real-Time Data Service**: The second type of service is to provide real-time data. The real-time data service is used to serve a variety of downstream applications. A few examples of such applications are mobile systems, real-time data provision to downstream applications such as **customer relationship management (CRM)** systems, recommendation engines on websites or mobile applications, and real-time outlier detection systems such fraud detection. A real-time data service manifests in multiple technology formats and adds tremendous business value if served correctly.

- **API-Based Data Service**: The third type of service used to share data are API-based data services. An API is an interface that allows applications to interact with an external service using a simple set of commands. Data can also be served as part of API interaction. As the data is exposed to multiple external services, API-based methods can scale to share data securely with external services. Data through an API is served in JSON format, therefore the technology used to serve the data using APIs should be able to support JSON formats. For example, a NoSQL database can store such data.

- **Data Sharing Service**: The fourth type of service is the data-sharing service. A data sharing data service shares data, in any format and any size, from multiple sources within an organization or other organizations. This type of service provides the required control to share data and allows data-sharing policies to be created. It also enables data sharing in a structured manner and offers complete visibility into how the data is shared and how it is used. A data-sharing system uses APIs for data sharing.

Data analytics layer

The data analytics layer involves the services that extract insights from data. They act as a playground for analysts, data scientists, and BI users to create reports, perform analysis, and experiment with AI/ML models. You can see the services that make us this layer in the following diagram:

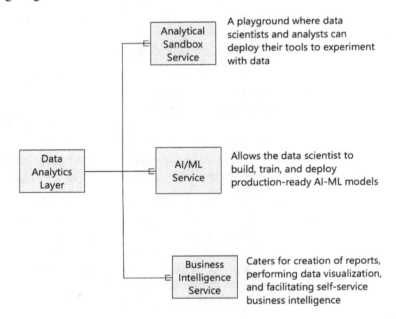

Figure 2.9 – Types of data analytics services

There are three types of services in the data analytics layer, outlined as follows:

- **Analytical Sandbox Service**: The analytical sandbox is a playground where data scientists and analysts can deploy their tools to experiment with data. The sandbox should provide different kinds of tools for SQL-based analysis and for developing ML models. This layer should also have seamless integration with the data lake layer and the data serving layer. This layer should spin up and shut down sets of tools on an on-demand basis to facilitate rapid experimentation.

- **Artificial Intelligence and Machine Learning (AI-ML) Service**: AI and ML services are vital components in a modern data analytics platform. The AI-ML service allows data scientists to build, train and deploy production-ready AI-ML models. This layer also provides the framework to maintain and monitor such models. In addition, it gives the ability for teams to collaborate as they go about building these models. This service should be able to scale up and down as required and should be able to facilitate automatic model deployment and operations.

- **Business Intelligence (BI) Service**: BI services have been around since the days of **enterprise data warehouses** (**EDWs**). In the data lakehouse architecture, they fulfill the same function. This service entails tools and technologies for creating reports, performing data visualization, and facilitating self-service BI. It is mainly focused on creating different tabular or visual views of the current and historical views of operations.

Data governance layer

The principle of *garbage in, garbage out* is also applicable for a data lakehouse. The data in a data lakehouse needs to be governed appropriately, and this layer looks after that. You can see a visual representation of it here:

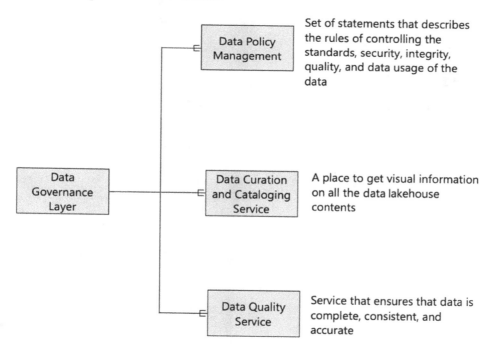

Figure 2.10 – Types of data governance services

Four components help to ensure that the data lakehouse does not become a data swamp. These are outlined as follows:

- **Data Policy Management**: The first component is not a technology component— it is a set of data policies and standards. A data policy is a set of statements that describe the rules of controlling the standards, security, integrity, quality, and usage of the data in the data lakehouse.

- **Data Cataloging and Curation Service**: Data cataloging and curation is the process of organizing an inventory of data so that it can be easily identified. This service ensures that all the source system data, data in the data lake and the data warehouse, the data processing pipelines, and the outputs extracted from the data lakehouse are appropriately cataloged. Think of data cataloging services as the Facebook of data—a place to get visual information on all of the data lakehouse's contents, including information about the relationships between the data and the lineage of transformations that the data has gone through.

- **Data Quality Service**: Any data stored or ingested in the data lakehouse must have a data quality score that determines the reliability and usability of the data. There are many parameters on which the quality of data is determined. A few of these parameters include the completeness of data, the consistency of data, and the accuracy of data. The data quality service ensures that data is complete, consistent, and accurate.

Data security layer

The final layer of the data lakehouse architecture is the data security layer. Data security is intense in itself, and its importance cannot be emphasized enough. You can see the services that make up this layer in the following diagram:

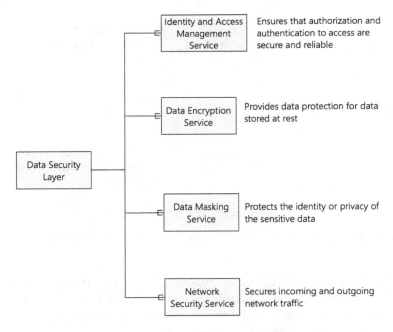

Figure 2.11 – Types of data security services

There are four critical components of the data security layer, as follows:

- **Identity and Access Management (IAM) Service**: The access to the data lakehouse must be secure and on a need basis. The IAM service acts as a gate for access to the data lakehouse. The IAM service ensures that authorization and authentication to access the data lakehouse are secure and reliable. It provides defense against malicious login attempts and safeguards credentials with risk-based access controls, identity protection tools, and robust authentication options—without disrupting productivity.

- **Data Encryption Service**: Data encryption is a security method where information is encoded and can only be accessed or decrypted by a user with the correct encryption key. Data encryption is essential when the data is stored in the cloud. Different kinds of algorithms are used to encrypt the data. Encryption provides data protection for data stored at rest. It prevents various types of cyber-attacks and protects sensitive data. Encryption of data may also be required by an organization's need for data governance and compliance efforts. Therefore, the data security layer needs to have the tools to encrypt and decrypt data as required.

- **Data Masking Service**: Many subsets of data need to be masked to protect the identity or privacy of the individual. This type of data includes emails, social identification numbers, credit card numbers, and so on. Data masking is a way to create a cryptic but readable version of data. The goal is to protect sensitive data while providing a functional alternative when actual data is not needed. The data security layer needs to have the tools to mask this sensitive data and unmask it as required.

- **Network Security Services**: The data in the Data Lakehouse needs to be secured all the time. The access to the data should be controlled such that any unauthorized access is denied. It also needs to be ensured that the data flowing between the external networks and the Data Lakehouse is secured. The network security service provides these functions.

This section provided an overview of the seven layers of a data lakehouse architecture. *Chapters 3 to 7* will cover these layers in detail. The chapters will elaborate on each of these layers and lay out common patterns that are used in practice.

Let's now move on to the architecture principles we will need to apply.

Developing architecture principles

As seen in the preceding section, many components make up a data lakehouse architecture. A data lakehouse architecture needs to be governed by a set of architecture principles that ensure that the data lakehouse can meet its goal of being a flexible platform for AI and BI and being agile to cater to ever-changing requirements.

Architecture principles govern any architectural construct and define the underlying general rules and guidelines for use. We can tailor these principles as per the organization's requirements. However, five principles are sacrosanct. These are represented in the following diagram:

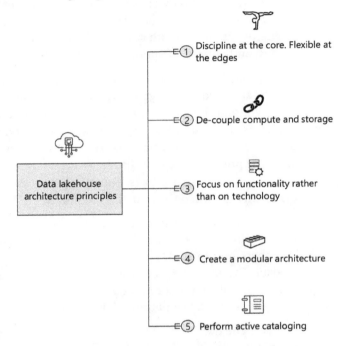

Figure 2.12 – Data lakehouse architecture principles

Disciplined at the core, flexible at the edges

The purpose of creating a new architecture paradigm is to be agile and innovative, yet it needs to be governed pragmatically. This balance is a fine line to tread. The first sacrosanct principle embodies that balance. Being disciplined at the core implies that the layers where data is stored need to be structured in their approach toward data management. These layers need to have detailed governance policies that leave no room for being ambiguous. However, the edges of the data lakehouse, the layers where data is transformed, forged, and made conducive to insights, need to be flexible. Flexibility doesn't mean being haywire in your approach. These layers are still governed within the policies of the data lakehouse. However, they exhibit certain flexibility for creating new features based on the demands of the requirements. An example of being flexible at the edge is mashing raw data from the data lake layer and data warehouse from the data serving layer to create an ML model. These datasets have different levels of quality scores and properties. However, such flexibility is acceptable as it facilitates rapid insight creation.

Decouple compute and storage

A data lakehouse stores a lot of data. It stores data in the data lake layer and the serving layer in structured and unstructured formats. The data needs to be processed with different types of compute engines. It can be a batch-based compute or a stream-based compute. A tightly coupled compute and storage layer strips off the flexibility required in a data lakehouse. Decoupling compute and storage also has a cost implication—storage is cheap and persistent but compute is expensive and ephemeral. It gives you the flexibility to spin up compute services on-demand and scale them as required, and also gives better cost control and cost predictability.

One of the critical challenges in the EDW and data lake pattern was the tight coupling of the compute and storage. The compute needs to be provisioned, whether it is being used or not. As the storage increases, the compute also needs to scale accordingly. **Cloud computing** platforms provide the flexibility of decoupling compute and storage.

Focus on functionality rather than technology

The next sacrosanct principle is to focus on the functionality of a component rather than its technological avatar. This principle embodies flexibility. As depicted in the system context diagram, a data lakehouse caters to many people. The technology manifestation of a data lakehouse has a plethora of technological choices. It can be deployed on any cloud platform or even on-premises using different types of choices. Also, technology is rapidly changing. Many new products are evolving commercially or in the open source world, focusing on fulfilling a specific functionality. Let's take real-time processing as an example. Apache Storm was a product released in 2011 that was optimized for real-time processing. Apache Spark, open sourced in 2010, gained traction as the de facto stream processing engine by 2013. Apache Spark evolved consistently, and Apache Flink is now challenging Apache Spark's supremacy as a stream processing engine. The technology evolution is rapid. However, the functionality remains the same—stream processing.

Focusing on one task that a component fulfills is essential. Furthermore, as technology evolves, we can easily replace the technology to meet the same functionality.

Create a modular architecture

A modular architecture refers to the design of any system composed of separate components that can connect. The beauty of modular architecture is that you can replace or add any part (module) without affecting the rest of the system.

A modular architecture ensures that a data lakehouse architecture is created flexibly, and we can add new functionality seamlessly without breaking existing functionality. For example, suppose there is a future requirement to add new functionality to the data lakehouse architecture. In that case, a component can be added such that it follows the same pattern as all other components. It gets data from the data lake layer, performs its functionality, and deposits the data into the processed data store for it to be served.

The modular architecture principle ensures that data stays at the core. Different services, based on their functionality, can be instantiated to use data as per the need.

Perform active cataloging

The single most important principle that prevents a data lakehouse from becoming a swamp is the degree of cataloging done within its layers. Thus, performing active cataloging is one of the sacrosanct principles. Cataloging is the key to preventing a data lake from becoming a data swamp. Diligent cataloging ensures that the users of the data lakehouse are **data-aware**. They should understand the properties of data stored in its various life stages. They need to understand the lineage of data's transformation journey, from its generation to its consumption. All the components that are part of the data lakehouse architecture need to be cataloged to provide a holistic view of the entire data life cycle with a data lakehouse.

Summary

This chapter was a 30,000-feet overview introduction to a data lakehouse architecture. This chapter started with the **system context** that established the critical systems and people that generate data for a data lakehouse and consume data from it. Next, we discussed the motivations and use cases for different types of data. Once the section clarified the system context, the chapter introduced the logical architecture of a data lakehouse. Next, the chapter provided a brief overview of the seven layers of a data lakehouse and its components. Finally, the chapter concluded with an elaboration of five sacrosanct architecture principles core to a robust data lakehouse architecture. The chapter lays the architectural foundation for a modern data analytics platform. Now that the stage is set, the subsequent chapters will go deeper into each of the layers and discuss design patterns for each layer.

In the next chapter, we will cover storing data in a data lakehouse.

Further reading

- *Developing a Data View (opengroup.org)*: http://www.opengroup.org/ public/arch/p4/views/vus_data.htm

- *Architectural Artifacts*: https://pubs.opengroup.org/architecture/ togaf9-doc/arch/chap31.html

- *Architecture Principles*: https://pubs.opengroup.org/architecture/ togaf8-doc/arch/chap29.html

- *System context diagram (Wikipedia)*: https://en.wikipedia.org/wiki/ System_context_diagram

- *Lambda architecture (Wikipedia)*: https://en.wikipedia.org/wiki/ Lambda_architecture

PART 2: Data Lakehouse Component Deep Dive

In this section of the book, we will explore the components of the data lakehouse architecture. The journey will begin with how data is ingested before moving on to how data is stored, served, cataloged, and converted into insights using analytics.

This section comprises the following chapters:

- *Chapter 3, Ingesting and Processing Data in a Data Lakehouse*
- *Chapter 4, Storing and Serving Data in a Data Lakehouse*
- *Chapter 5, Deriving Insights from a Data Lakehouse*
- *Chapter 6, Applying Data Governance in a Data Lakehouse*
- *Chapter 7, Applying Data Security in a Data Lakehouse*

3
Ingesting and Processing Data in a Data Lakehouse

In the previous chapter, we provided an overview of the architectural components of a data lakehouse. That chapter provided a bird's-eye view of the seven layers and described these layers in considerable detail. This chapter will cover the architectural patterns for the first two layers of a data lakehouse:

- The data ingestion layer
- The data processing layer

These two layers need to be covered together as they are interlinked. Data is relayed from the ingestion layer to the processing layer. Many of the tools and technologies that are used in both these layers are the same.

This chapter is divided into five sections. We will start by exploring the differences between the **extract, transform, load** (**ETL**) and **extract, load, transform** (**ELT**) data transformation patterns. Then, we will dive deeper into the methods for ingesting and processing batch data. After that, we will do the same for streaming data. Finally, we will discuss the **Lambda** architectural pattern, which combines batch and stream processing.

In this chapter, we will cover the following topics:

- Ingesting and processing batch data
- Ingesting and processing streaming data
- Bringing it all together

Ingesting and processing batch data

Let's start by looking at the logical architecture of a data lakehouse:

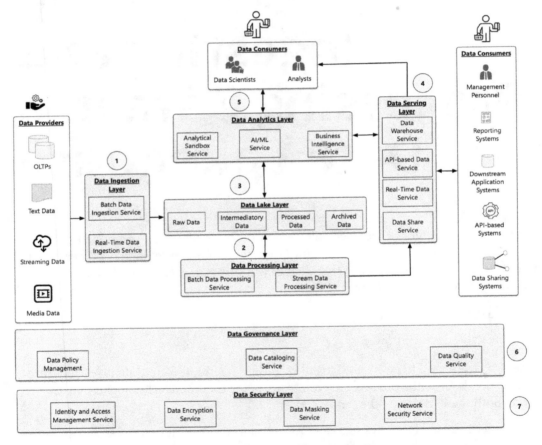

Figure 3.1 – Data lakehouse logical architecture

The preceding diagram depicts the seven logical layers. Data from the data providers needs to be ingested and transformed. Traditionally, there are two types of batch data ingestion and transformation patterns:

- ETL
- ELT

Understanding these patterns is vital if you wish to understand how they can be combined for batch ingestion and processing in a data lakehouse.

Let's discuss these patterns in detail.

Differences between the ETL and ELT patterns

Let's discuss the differences between these patterns in detail. On the surface, these patterns may seem similar. However, there are differences in their philosophy and the services that are employed to transform data.

ETL

The first pattern is ETL. The following diagram depicts a typical ETL pattern:

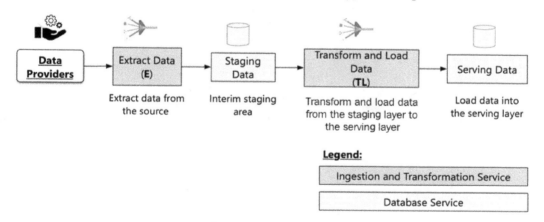

Figure 3.2 – ETL pattern

This pattern entails the following stages:

1. **Extract**: Extract any data from the data sources and load it into a staging area. The staging area is transient and interim: data from the staging area is purged after each batch load. The staging area also ensures that the source is decoupled. An **ETL tool** is used to connect to the source and **pull** the data into the staging area. Another method is to **push** the data into a repository. From there, it can be extracted and staged.

2. **Transform**: Once the data lands in the staging area, the ETL tool transforms the data. While the data is being transformed, the computing power of the ETL tool is used. This process implies that the transformation's speed and scale depend on the server configuration of the ETL tools.

3. **Load**: Once the data has been transformed, it is loaded into the serving data layer. This task is performed by the ETL tool as well.

As is evident from this process, in the ETL pattern, the onus of ingestion and data transformation service is on an ETL tool. The database service doesn't perform any transformations. Another point to note is that the ETL tool is also tightly integrated with the database that it loads the data into.

ELT

The second pattern is ELT. The following diagram depicts a typical ELT pattern:

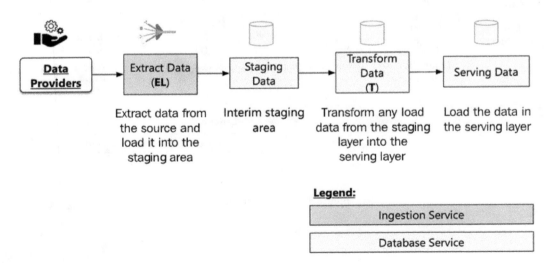

Figure 3.3 – ELT pattern

This pattern entails the following stages:

1. **Extract**: Like the ETL pattern, the ELT tool extracts data from the data sources and loads it into a staging area. This staging area is transient and interim. This area ensures that the source is decoupled. Again, it can be a push or pull methodology for extracting data into the staging area.

2. **Load-Transform**: Once the data is in the staging area, data transformation is performed using the database's compute engine. The more compute power that's used from the database engine, the faster the data transformation process will be.

In the ELT pattern, the onus of ingestion is on the ELT tool. The database engine transforms and loads the data. This type of pattern uses the power of the database engine to perform the required transformations. This pattern is very prevalent in data lakes that use the Hadoop ecosystem for ELT and **massively parallel processing** (**MPP**) architecture-based databases.

Batch data processing in a data lakehouse

The batch data processing that's performed in a data lakehouse combines both the ETL and ELT patterns. It weaves a pattern called the **extract, load, transform, load** (**ELTL**) pattern. The ELTL pattern **decouples each functionality**. Thus, each function is fulfilled by one, and only one, service.

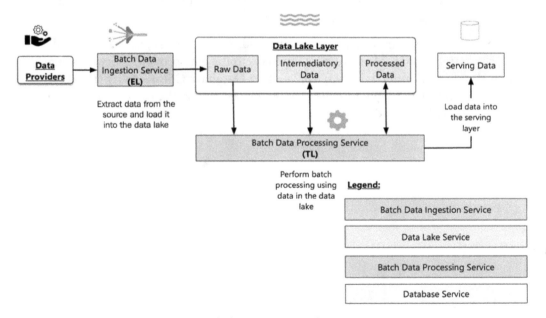

Figure 3.4 – Batch data ingestion and processing pattern

The preceding diagram depicts a typical ELTL pattern. The ingestion service is used to ingest the data into the data lake. The data lake service is used to store data persistently. As the data is transformed, intermediatory datasets are also stored in the data lake. The batch processing service processes the data, and selective data is served downstream using the data serving service. The data ingestion and processing services are on-demand and are only active during the time of processing. Let's delve deeper into this pattern.

Extract-load

The first step entails extracting the data from the data provider and loading it into the raw data layer in the data lake. Unlike other patterns, the raw data store is **persistent**. The data is stored in this layer for a longer duration. The data is also true to its natural form and doesn't undergo any transformation. As expected, the onus of extraction and load is on the **ingestion service**. The ingestion service is **on-demand** and is activated when the data from the source becomes available for extraction. The raw data store also ensures that the right level of decoupling is achieved between the data provider and the data lake.

As depicted in the following diagram, the data is ingested into the raw data store using either a push or a pull methodology. The **push** methodology uses the **file transfer protocol (FTP)** or a program written in programming languages such as Python or Java to push the data into the data lake. The program is controlled by the data providers and may be scheduled to run periodically. It pushes the data provider's data to the data lake layer and decouples the source and the data lake. The data provider also controls the security and the outbound networking ports to be opened.

Another method that's employed is the **pull** method. As its name suggests, in the pull method, the extract-load tool or program connects to the data provider's database using the **Open Database Connectivity (ODBC)** or **Java Database Connectivity (JDBC)** methods. Inbound networking ports need to be opened so that the program can connect to the database. Both methods are illustrated in the following diagram:

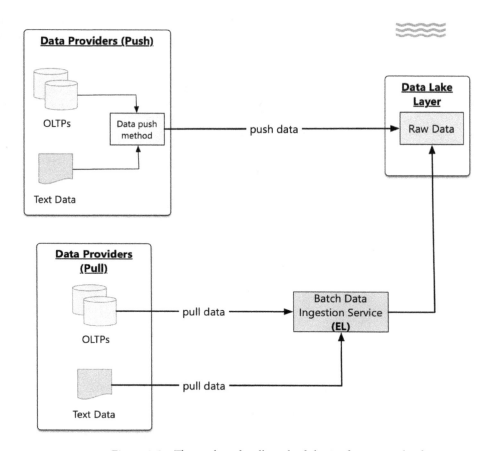

Figure 3.5 – The push and pull methodologies for extract-load

Let us now discuss the process of transform-load.

Transform-load

The next step in the ELTL process is to **transform-load** the data. A modern data engineering strategy employs a distributed computing framework for data transformation. A distributed computing framework has become the de facto technology that is used for big data processing. Distributed data processing uses parallelism to process data faster and at scale. The preceding diagram depicts a typical distributed data processing pattern.

The following diagram depicts the framework for distributed computing that is used in batch data processing:

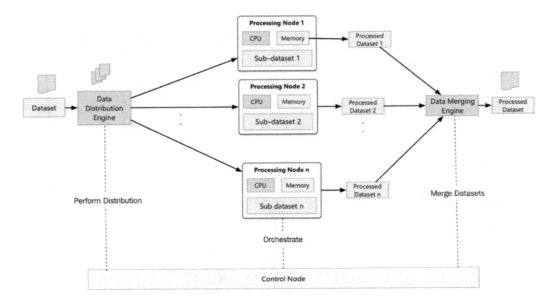

Figure 3.6 – The distributed batch data processing framework

The following are the key steps for implementing distributed batch processing:

1. A dataset is distributed into multiple smaller datasets using an appropriate distribution strategy. Two key distribution strategies are as follows:

    I.   **Hash distribution**: A hash distribution partitions data based on a hashing function that's applied to a specific column.

    II. **Round robin distribution**: In a round-robin distribution, the data is distributed across multiple partitions, which is then distributed into partitions without any optimization. Each row is assigned to a partition sequentially.

2. Once the data has been distributed using the appropriate distribution strategies, the larger dataset is splintered into multiple smaller ones. Now, here is where the magic of parallelism happens. Each subset of data gets its own compute unit. This dedicated compute unit transforms that specific subset. A typical **compute unit** will have CPU and memory assigned to process a subset of the data. To speed up processing, more and more compute nodes can be added as required. This process is called **horizontal scaling (scale-out)**. The computing power in each compute unit can also be increased by allocating more memory or more CPU cores to the node. This process is called **vertical scaling (scale-up)**.

3. Each compute node transforms its subset of data and creates a processed dataset. Finally, the processed datasets from each compute node are merged into a single processed dataset.

4. The actions of distributing the data, orchestrating between the different compute nodes, and eventually merging the data is performed by the control node.

A batch data processing service employs a distributed computing framework for processing the data and propagating it through the **intermediatory data store** and the **processed data store** in the data lake layer. The service is on-demand and can be scaled as and when required. In addition, a selective copy of any data that needs to be served downstream is also loaded into the serving layer.

Now that we've learned how batch data is ingested and processed, let's learn how streaming data is ingested and processed.

Ingesting and processing streaming data

The following diagram depicts the components required for stream data ingestion and processing:

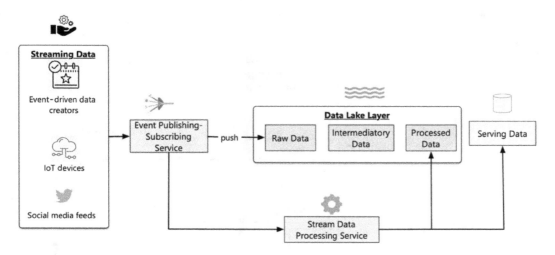

Figure 3.7 – The streaming data ingestion and processing pattern

Now, let's discuss how to stream data processing through the lens of the ELTL process.

Streaming data sources

Streaming data is a data source that continuously emanates data. Social media feeds, IoT devices, and event-driven processes such as swiping a credit card are examples of streaming data. The data is continually produced, and the goal of stream processing is to tap into that stream of data and gain insights as quickly as possible. Stream data ingestion and processing facilitate real-time analytics. This implies that analytics is performed on the data without the data being persisted on disk.

Extraction-load

Stream data is extracted using an event publishing-subscribing service. An event publishing-subscribing service enables creating a system in which you can publish the messages or events into various topics. It also allows you to subscribe to these topics for processing. The service acts like a messaging middleware that enables horizontal and vertical scaling. The messages are stored in the topics for the subscription. The stream processing engine can tap into these topics and transform the events, as shown in the following diagram:

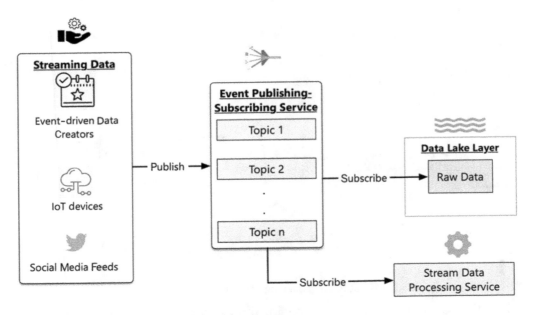

Figure 3.8 – Stream publishing-subscribing service

The service also enables the messages to be persisted in the raw data store part of the data lake. The service ensures that a copy of the raw data is maintained, even if the data from the topics is purged.

Transform-load

Now, let's see how streaming data can be transformed and loaded so that it can be served.

Once the data has been ingested in the event publishing-subscribing service, the transformation process for stream data has two stages: **micro-batching** and **action**.

The following diagram shows how a stream is transformed:

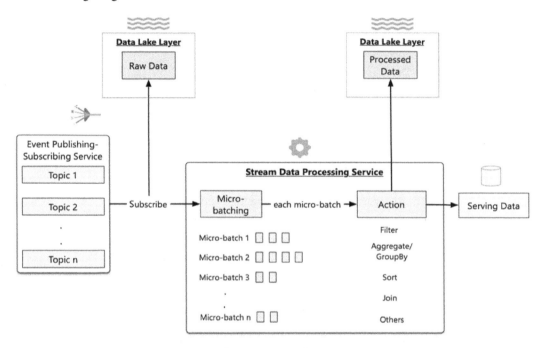

Figure 3.9 – The stream transformation process

Micro-batching

The first stage is called micro-batching. Micro-batching is the process of collecting small sets of data from a stream and performing transformations on that set. The micro-batching strategy can be time-based, such as collecting stream data for a prescribed set of time, or it can be event-based, in that you could collect stream data until a prescribed event happens. Let's discuss each micro-batching method in detail.

Time-based micro-batching

In a time-based micro-batching process, the incoming events are processed based on a specific period. Depending on how fast the events need to be processed, this time window can be shortened or extended. When the specified time window lapses, the events that have been collected within this window are sent to the next stage of transform-load: the action stage. The following diagram depicts the process of time-based micro-batching:

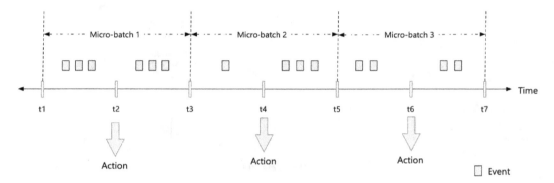

Figure 3.10 – Time-based micro-batching

Time-based micro-batching is used when the event stream is consistent and there is no focus on a specific type of event. An example of this micro-batching can be collecting tweets that have a particular hashtag during a period of, say, 10 seconds. In this example, the focus is not on a specific event but on a collection of events (tweets with a particular hashtag) that occurred over a certain period (for example, a period of 10 seconds). The length of the window is constant. There are many variations of time-based micro-batching:

- A **tumbling window** collects events over a fixed set of times.
- A **hopping window** collects events over a fixed set of time, but the windows move by a pre-determined period as well.

Event-based micro-batching

In event-based micro-batching, the period is secondary. The focus of micro-batching is on an event of interest. When that event of interest occurs, a micro-batch is created for that specific event or all the events between the two occurrences of interest. These micro-batches can vary in time. The following diagram depicts event-based micro-batching:

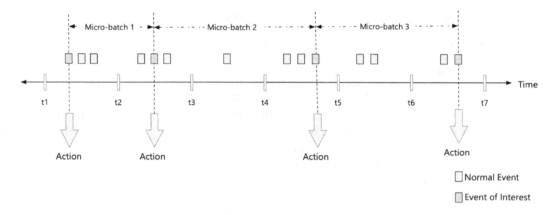

Figure 3.11 – Event-based micro-batching

Event-based micro-batching is used when an action needs to be performed when an event of interest is encountered. This micro-batch can only be consistent with the event of interest or all the events between the events of interest. Let's look at two examples that illustrate event-based micro-batching.

Flagging a tweet with a profane word is a form of event-based micro-batching that consists of only one event, which is the event of interest (the tweet containing the offensive word). When such an event occurs, an action is triggered on the specific tweet.

An example of event-based micro-batching that involves multiple events is collecting clicks on a website when a specific marketing ad is displayed. Potentially, all the clicks that occurred during the ad periods shown can be attributed to the advertisement.

Action

Now that we have explained what micro-batching is, let's discuss various actions that you can perform on this micro batch. There are generally two types of actions that you can perform on a micro batch: **grouping-based actions** and **event-based actions**.

Grouping-based actions

As its name suggests, a grouping-based action applies specific transformations to the collection of events within the micro batch. Common types of grouping-based actions are as follows:

- **Filtering**: Filter the micro-batch based on specific conditions.
- **Aggregate**: Apply aggregation functions such as sum, average, and mean.

- **Sort**: Sort the micro-batch streams based on specific sort values.
- **Join**: Join the micro-batch data with other datasets.

Event-based actions

Event-based actions perform actions on a specific event. This can be a simple action such as immediately triggering some logic or a complex action such as running the event through a series of rules to determine subsequent actions for that event or passing the event through a machine learning model to predict or determine outcomes. The key concept to note here is that event-based actions are performed on one event of interest, not on a group of events.

Once the micro-batches have been transformed, the resultant datasets are **loaded** into two places. First, one copy of the resulting dataset is loaded into the processed data store of the data lake. Second, another copy of the resultant dataset is loaded into the serving database.

Bringing it all together

So far, we have covered the essential elements of batch and stream ingestion and processing. Now, let's bring these two types of processing together to define the **Lambda** architecture pattern.

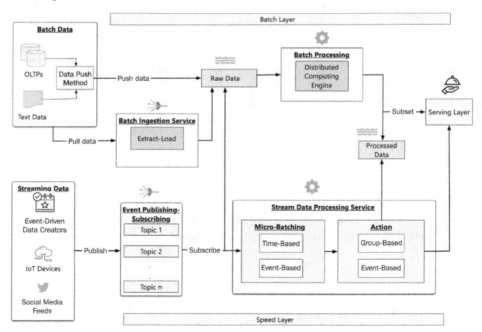

Figure 3.12 – Lambda architecture pattern

The preceding diagram depicts a Lambda architecture pattern. A Lambda architecture pattern has three layers: the **batch layer**, the **speed layer**, and the **serving layer**.

The batch layer

The following diagram illustrates batch layer processing in a Lambda architecture:

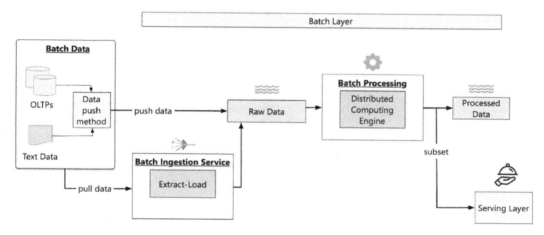

Figure 3.13 – The batch layer in a Lambda architecture

Batch layer processing consists of ingesting the data into the **raw data store** of the data lake using pull or push methodologies through a **batch data ingestion service**. Once the data has been ingested in the raw data store, a **batch processing service** is initiated. The batch processing service employs a **distributed computing engine** for faster data processing. The processed data is then served in two places. First, it goes to the **processed data store** of the data lake. Then, it goes to a component in the **serving layer** that is used for downstream consumption.

The speed layer

The following diagram illustrates speed layer processing in a Lambda architecture:

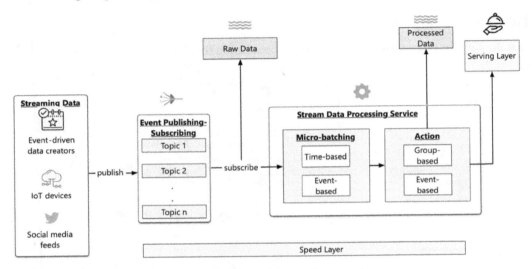

Figure 3.14 – The speed layer in a Lambda architecture

The speed layer processes the streaming data. The streaming data is ingested by being published to one of the topics of the **event publishing service**. The raw data is also pushed into the **raw data store** of the data lake layer. The **stream processing service** subscribes to the topics and processes the stream in micro batches and performs specific actions either on a group of events or on a single event of interest. The processed data is then served in two places. First, it goes to the **processed data store** of the data lake. Then, it goes to a component in the **serving layer** that is used for downstream consumption.

The serving layer

The serving layer is used to **serve** the processed data to downstream consumers. Based on the need and the non-functional requirements of the downstream consumers, you can serve the data in multiple forms and methods. The serving layer will be covered in more depth in *Chapter 5, Deriving Insights from a Data Lakehouse.*

Summary

This chapter covered data ingestion and processing. We started by exploring the different patterns for batch data ingestion: ETL and ELT.

Then, we delved into the different components of the ELTL pattern, which is used to ingest and process batch data in a data lakehouse. Then, we discussed how to push or pull data into a raw data store. Finally, we discussed the pivotal role that the raw data store layer plays in data ingestion and processing.

Next, we delved into distributed computing and how it is used for processing batch data at scale.

After discussing batch data ingestion and processing, we discussed patterns for ingesting and processing stream data. Then, we discussed how to ingest stream data by publishing it to a topic and subscribing to it for processing. Finally, we learned how to micro batch the streams and exercise actions on a micro batch or a specific event of interest.

Finally, we brought all the concepts we'd discussed together and weaved them into a Lambda architecture. Here, we discussed the methods by which batch layers and speed layers can be realized.

Data ingestion and processing are essential in any modern data analytics platform. Without an efficiently designed data ingestion and processing layer, the entire architecture can fail to deliver the expected outcome. This chapter provided practical design patterns that can be employed for architecting a modern data analytics platform to make data ingestion and processing scalable and adaptable.

In the next chapter, we will focus on how to store data in a data lake.

Further reading

For more information regarding the topics that were covered in this chapter, take a look at the following resources:

- **Massively Parallel** on *Wikipedia*: https://en.wikipedia.org/wiki/Massively_parallel

- *Welcome to Azure Stream Analytics*: https://docs.microsoft.com/en-us/azure/stream-analytics/stream-analytics-introduction

- *Introduction to Stream Analytics windowing functions*: https://docs.microsoft.com/en-us/azure/stream-analytics/stream-analytics-window-functions

- *HDFS Architecture Guide*: https://hadoop.apache.org/docs/r1.2.1/hdfs_design.html

- *Evaluation of distributed stream processing frameworks for IoT applications in Smart Cities* (2019), by Hamid Nasiri, Saeed Nasehi, and Maziar Goudarzi, in *Journal of Big Data*: `https://journalofbigdata.springeropen.com/articles/10.1186/s40537-019-0215-2`

- *A Comparative Study on Streaming Frameworks for Big Data* (2018,) by Wissem Inoubli, Sabeur Aridhi, Haithem Mezni, Mondher Maddouri, and Engelbert Mephu Nguifo, in *Latin America Data Science Workshop*: `http://ceur-ws.org/Vol-2170/paper3.pdf`

- *A Survey of Distributed Data Stream Processing Frameworks* (2019), by Haruna Isah, Tariq Abughofa, Sazia Mahfuz, Dharmitha Ajerla, Farhana Zulkernine, and Shahzad Khan, in *IEEE Access*: `https://ieeexplore.ieee.org/document/8864052`

- *What Is Lambda Architecture? - Databricks*: `https://databricks.com/glossary/lambda-architecture`

4
Storing and Serving Data in a Data Lakehouse

The journey so far has covered a lot of ground, storing data in a data lake is the new architecture paradigm for data architecture. The first chapter covered trends in big data and discussed the need for a new paradigm. The second chapter provided an overview of the **data lakehouse** architecture and discussed the seven layers of a data lakehouse. The third chapter focused on the methods in which data can be ingested and processed in a data lakehouse. In this chapter, we will focus on storing the data in the data lake and the *data serving* layers of the data lakehouse architecture.

Data storage is critical from both a storage and performance perspective. This chapter will begin by providing a view of how data is stored in the *data lake* layer. Next, we will discuss the different data stores within a data lake, along with their needs and benefits. We will then explore the standard data formats used for storing data in a data lake. Finally, we will focus on storing data in the *data serving* layer for various instances of downstream consumption. This chapter will cover multiple architectural patterns for serving data for **SQL**-based contexts, and we will also cover **NoSQL**-based data serving.

In summary, this chapter will cover the following topics:

- Storing data in the data lake layer
- Storing data in the data serving layer

Storing data in the data lake layer

Once the data is ingested into the *data lake* layer, it needs to be managed and stored correctly. A resilient storage strategy reduces the unnecessary duplication of data. In addition, it ensures that need-based access is provided for the stakeholders and that proper security controls are applied to ensure data security. So, let's first investigate the various datastores of a data lake.

Data lake layer

Data in the data lake layer is segregated into multiple datastores. Each datastore has its own purpose and guidelines for use. As depicted in the following figure, there are four types of datastores in the *data lake* layer:

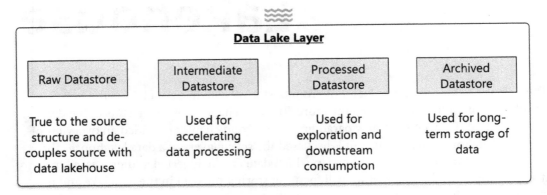

Figure 4.1 – The types of datastores in a data lake

The data in the data lake is stored in a *hierarchical file structure*. A hierarchical file structure creates a folder that behaves more like a traditional operating system's filesystem in terms of moving and renaming files. In addition, it facilitates fine-grain **Role-Based Access Control (RBAC)** at the directory and sub-directory levels.

The levels of a hierarchical filesystem are depicted in the following figure:

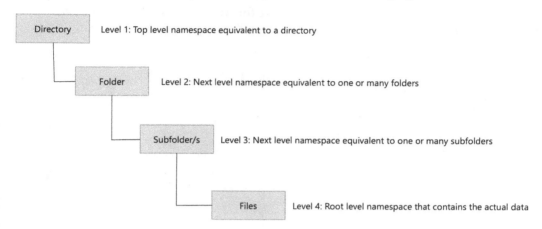

Figure 4.2 – The hierarchical file system structure

The top level is the directory that contains one or more folders. Each directory can include one or more folders that form the second level. Each folder has one or more subfolders, and the actual data files are stored in the subfolders.

The hierarchical filesystem enables data to be partitioned and stored efficiently. It also ensures the faster retrieval of data if the underlying data is partitioned based on folders and subfolders.

The data lake's *raw*, *intermediate*, and *processed* datastores are stored in a hierarchical file organization. However, the *archival* datastore, which is meant for long-term storage, may or may not be stored in the hierarchical file system.

Now, let's investigate each of these datastores/layers in detail.

The raw datastore

The following figure shows how the *raw* datastore forms the first destination for data entering the data lake:

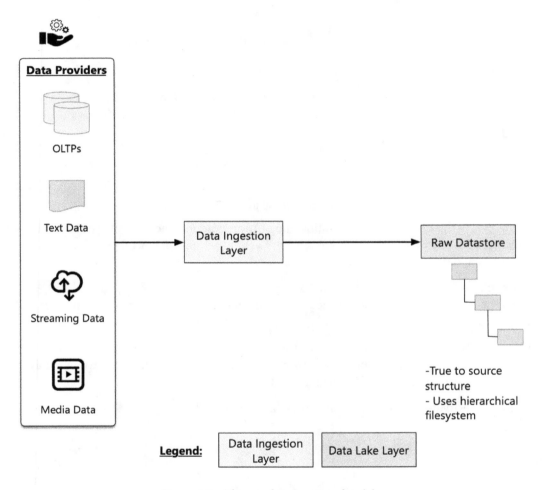

Figure 4.3 – The raw datastore in a data lake

The raw datastore is the landing zone that de-couples sources from the data lakehouse. The data from the source is stored in the raw datastore in data formats that are suited to big data processing. Examples of these formats include **CSV**, **Apache Parquet**, and **JSON**.

From a structural perspective, the data structure in the raw datastore is the same as that of the sources. This principle implies that the rows and columns found in the source data are preserved when it lands in the raw datastore.

If the source data is unstructured, data format is preserved. For example, if the image is a *JPEG* file, it is copied to the data lake datastore in the `.jpg` format. The *raw* datastore is also called the *bronze* datastore.

The intermediate datastore

The second destination is the *intermediate* datastore. The following figure shows the data movement from the **Raw Datastore** to the **Intermediate Datastore**:

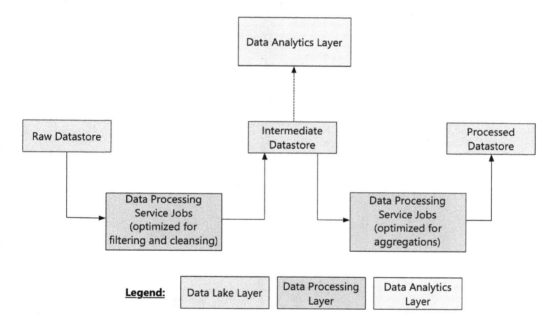

Figure 4.4 – The intermediate datastore in a data lake

Once the data lands in the raw datastore, it needs to be processed. When the raw data is processed, it goes through many intermediate stages. For example, data in the raw datastore can be cleaned, filtered, aggregated, appended, and so on. These are referred to as the *intermediate* stages of data processing. It is wise to store these intermediate files for two key reasons:

- First, we can use these intermediate datasets if the processing jobs need to be restarted.

- Second, the intermediate datastore acts as a source for the processed datastore.

We can use optimized compute power to process data from the *intermediate* to the *processed* datastore. The segregation of datastores ensures that the correct type of computing process is applied to raw data. The *intermediate* datastore is also called the *silver* datastore.

The processed datastore

The third data store in the data lake layer is the *processed* datastore. As depicted in the following figure, the processed datastore is the last *active* (that is used for data processing) layer in the data lake:

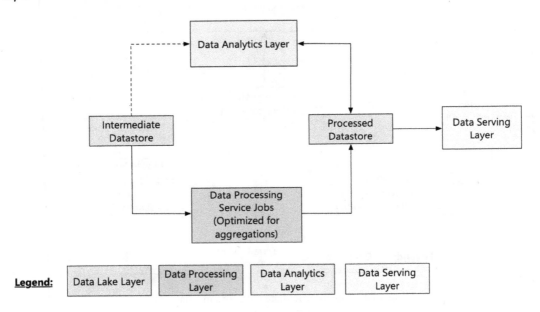

Figure 4.5 – The processed datastore in a data lake

The data in the intermediate datastore is aggregated and stored in the processed datastore. The processed datastore is the layer where data is already cleansed, aggregated, and ready to be served. The data is then processed, and the processed datastore can also be accessed by the *data analytics* layer for analytics activities such as data exploration, ad hoc queries, machine learning, and so on.

The *processed* datastore is also called the *gold* datastore.

The archived datastore

The final layer in the data lake is the *archived* datastore. Many organizations require the data to be stored for long-term purposes. Archived datastores provide storage for such requirements. In addition, the data in the archived datastore is generally stored in a cheaper storage technology that doesn't require fast retrieval times (also referred to as **input/output**).

As shown in the following figure, an archiving schedule is set and periodically triggered to transfer data from the *raw*, *intermediate*, or *processed* datastores into the *archived* datastore for long-term storage. To maintain an acceptable price-performance balance, retrieving data from arrival storage is slower than the other datastores because the data is stored in cheaper storage technology. Therefore, it is wise to set an appropriate archiving schedule and ensure that only data that is no longer actively required is archived.

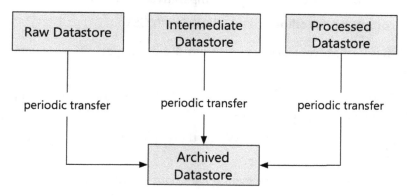

Figure 4.6 – The archived datastore in a data lake

Now that we have covered the different layers of the data lake, let's explore some of the common data formats used in data lakes.

Common data formats

In this section, we will discuss common data formats that are used to store both structured and unstructured data within data lakes.

The CSV format

The **Comma-Separated Values (CSV)** format is a prevalent format for data storage.

A CSV file is essentially a delimited text file that stores **tabular data**. This file uses a comma to separate data between fields. The comma is called the *delimiter*. The files can use other types of delimiters, such as pipes (|) or tabs (_). The CSV format has been around for decades and is still widely used for data storage. There are advantages and disadvantages to storing data in the CSV format. The key benefits of storing data in CSV files are as follows:

- CSV has a schema and is human-readable, making it easy to edit manually.
- CSV implementation is relatively simple, and it is an easy format to parse.
- CSV is faster to handle as the files are comparatively small in size.
- Various **compaction methods** can work well with CSV.

However, CSV has its disadvantages as well. A few disadvantages of storing data in CSV are as follows:

- The CSV structure mainly supports text data. CSV does not support complex data structures such as arrays or binaries.
- Data is stored as simple text in a CSV file; there is no distinction between text and numeric values.
- There is no standard way to represent binary data in CSV.
- CSV has poor support for special characters, and there is no standard way to represent control characters.

The Parquet format

In a row-based file format such as CSV, data is stored as rows. However, row-oriented storage is not optimized for analytics, as every row needs to be scanned to fetch a specific value. When compared to row-based storage, column-based storage is more suited for analytical workloads. Data stored as columns significantly reduces the data fetched from the disk when queried because the query will retrieve only the relevant columns. Column-based storage also combines efficient encoding and compression methods to reduce storage requirements without compromising query performance. **Parquet** is an open source, column-based storage format available to any project in the **Apache Hadoop** ecosystem. The Parquet file format is optimized for big data workloads. It is built from the ground up to support very efficient compression and encoding schemes.

The Parquet format has distinct advantages to the CSV format. The key benefits of the Parquet format are as follows:

- Parquet is designed to improve efficiency for storage and querying compared to row-based storage such as CSV.

- One of the disadvantages of CSV files is their inability to handle complex nested structures. Parquet can support these complex data structures. In addition, the layout of Parquet data files is optimized for queries that process large volumes of data (in the gigabyte range) for each file.

- As mentioned, one other disadvantage of CSV is its limited options for compression methods. On the other hand, Parquet has many flexible compression options and efficient encoding schemes that result in efficient storage optimization.

- Parquet also works well when we need to query the underlying data in an ad hoc and interactive manner.

The JSON format

When it comes to storing semi-structured data, **JavaScript Object Notation (JSON)** is frequently the format that is used. JSON is an open standard file format and data interchange format. It stores data in human-readable text and is commonly used as the main format for data interchange, including on the web.

Other formats

Data lakes can also store unstructured data such as videos, images, audio files, and text. Some of the standard formats used for each of them are as follows:

- **Video**: **MPEG-4 Part 14** (otherwise known as **MP4**) file formats for video have been around for a long time. An MP4 format can store many data structures in smaller file formats, including audio files, video files, still images, and text.

- **Images**: The **Joint Photographic Experts Group (JPEG)**, **Tagged Image File Format (TIFF)**, and **Graphics Interchange Format (GIF)** formats are common file formats used for images.

- **Audio**: The **Waveform Audio File Format (WAV)** and **Audio Video Interleave (AVI)** formats are standard audio data formats.

Now that we have covered the storage formats used in the data lake layer, let's investigate another aspect of data storage – that is, storing data in the *data serving* layer.

Storing data in the data serving layer

Once the data is processed in the data lake, it needs to be *served* to the downstream applications or stakeholders. The following figure shows the interaction between different data lake layers and the data serving layer:

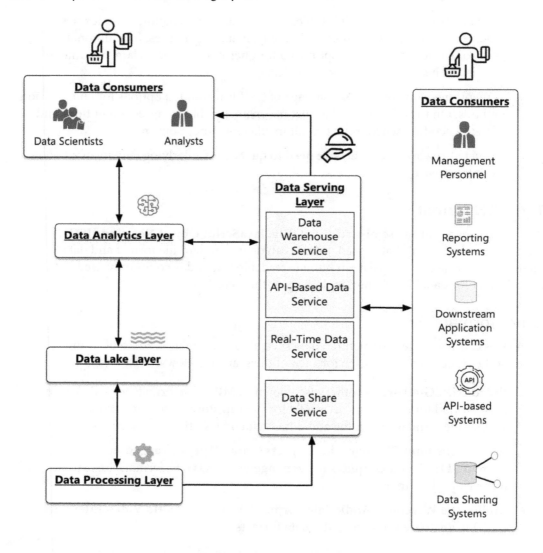

Figure 4.7 – The interaction of other data lake layers with the data serving layer

Let's investigate the different datastores that we can use in the data serving layer to enable these services.

The following figure maps how the different datastores can be utilized using different technologies:

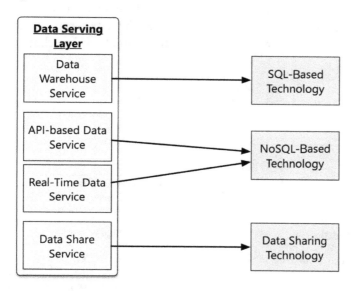

Figure 4.8 – Mapping the data serving layer to different technologies

Now, let's move on to cover SQL-based serving.

SQL-based serving

Relational Database Management Systems (RDBMSes) have been used to store structured data for many decades. They still have their place in the context of modern data analytics. **Structured Query Language (SQL)**, the language for communicating with an RDBMS, is widely used for querying data.

SQL-based databases are used as the data serving layer. They can come in the form of data warehouses or data marts, which are typically used for reporting, data analysis, and self-service analysis. Depending on the system's query performance and cost optimization, two types of SQL-based databases can be employed as the data serving layer. The following figure illustrates the two types of SQL-based databases and their key characteristics:

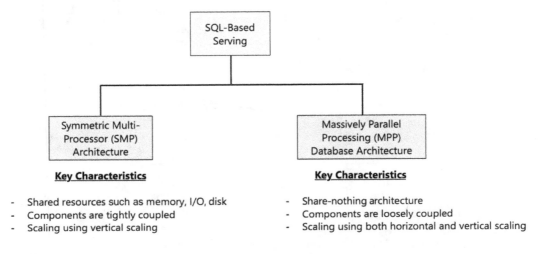

Figure 4.9 – Different types of SQL-based data serving layers

Let's investigate each of these in detail.

SMP-based architecture

The first type of SQL-based serving database is based on **Symmetric Multi-Processor (SMP) architecture**. This technology comprises compute, storage, and network elements. These building blocks have evolved so much that SMP-driven databases can now support small-to-medium-scale analytical requirements for a commendable price. The following figure depicts the logical architecture of an SMP-based RDBMS:

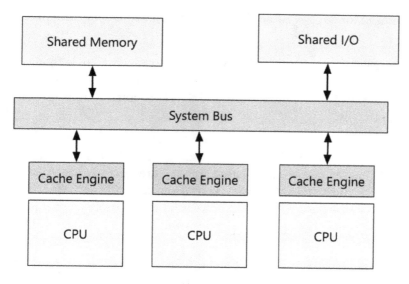

Figure 4.10 – SMP logical architecture

An SMP-based RDBMS has shared resources such as memory, I/O, operating systems, and disks. SMP is a tightly coupled architecture. The way to scale it is using **vertical scaling** – that is, increasing the memory or the CPUs. There are some inherent advantages to using SMP-based architecture, and a few of them are as follows:

- **Network speed**: All SMP components are essentially contained in one server. This fusion implies that there is no latency when communicating between the components.

- **No data shuffling**: Since the data is stored in one location, there is no need to shuffle the data, which improves latency.

- **Fewer failure points**: SMP is a tightly coupled architecture. Its CPU, memory, and I/O are fused and work as a single unit. Therefore, it has fewer points of failure.

- **Faster updates**: As the data is consistent within the SMP architecture, it stands out when there are requirements for frequent updates. The SMP architecture can effectively apply all of the constructs of an RDBMS, such as **Atomicity, Consistency, Isolation**, and **Durability (ACID)** properties, database triggers, indexes, and more, all within an SMP system.

However, when used for large-scale analytics, the SMP-based architecture inherits challenges as well:

- **Performance**: Data analytics has become a large-scale domain, with petabytes of data involved. The CPU and memory have their limits in a single server. As the data volume grows, SMP's monolithic and tightly coupled architecture fails to perform optimally.

- **Scalability**: Modern data analytics demands scalability and elasticity in computing. The data serving layer needs to scale depending on the type of query and the consumer using the system. SMP-based architecture can only scale vertically. This scalability constraint limits the ability to scale on-demand because scaling based on the CPU or RAM usage is limited. If we want to add more storage or CPUs, the SMP-based data serving layer needs downtime for an upgrade, which can be disruptive.

- **Cost**: As the data volume grows, achieving an acceptable performance level at an optimal price point becomes a challenge with SMP architecture.

- **Maintainability**: As mentioned earlier, the monolithic nature of SMP architecture means that it presents a single point of failure. As resilience is not built-in, SMP-based architecture needs more maintenance to ensure high availability.

Microsoft SQL Server, **Oracle**, **MySQL**, and **Postgres DB** are a few examples of SMP databases.

Now, let's dive into another type of SQL-based data serving layer that is predominantly used in modern data analytics architecture.

MPP-based architecture

Massively Parallel Processing (**MPP**)-based architecture takes a different approach to dealing with data and employs a *share-nothing* style of architecture. The following figure depicts a typical example of logical architecture in an MPP context:

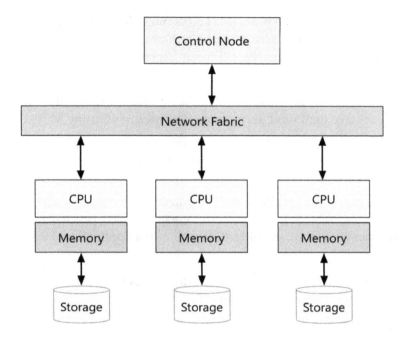

Figure 4.11 – MPP logical architecture

MPP architecture slices the data into multiple chunks and processes each chunk independently. Each processing unit has its memory, CPU, and storage. A control node acts as a director and assigns what will be processed by each processing unit. The control node also performs other functions, such as consolidating the data from multiple processing units. The key features of MPP are as follows:

- MPP employs a *share-nothing* style of architecture, and each processing unit has its own set of RAM, CPU, and storage resources. Furthermore, each processing unit performs its processing of the queries (for example, aggregations, filtering, and more).

- MPP architecture is both horizontally and vertically scalable. Just by increasing the capacity of a node, it can be vertically scaled. MPP can also be horizontally scaled by adding a new processing unit to the architecture.

- Data is partitioned and distributed across multiple storage nodes. A single processing unit acts upon each storage node. When the storage is cloud-based, the underlying physical storage is partitioned into logical storage units.

Because the data is distributed and processed across multiple units, MPP is suited to performing analytics on large datasets. As a result, there are significant advantages of using MPP over SMP in big data analytics. The key benefits of MPP-based architecture are as follows:

- **Performance**: As MPP architecture can be scaled both horizontally and vertically, it is easier to achieve significant performance improvements using MPP.

- **Scalability**: MPP can scale seamlessly as more nodes are added to it. Typically, MPP enables scaling by adding new nodes without downtime. SMP cannot achieve this level of seamless scalability.

- **Cost**: Cost is more manageable in MPP architecture. Performing analytics on large datasets with SMP becomes cost-prohibitive, as the system gets more expensive with significant memory. However, with MPP, scaling at an optimal cost is not a problem, as new nodes can be added and scaled horizontally.

Despite these advantages, there are also a few disadvantages to an MPP-based data serving layer. Some of the disadvantages are as follows:

- **Network speed**: All the nodes of an MPP-based data serving layer are connected to the network fabric. Therefore, the connection may introduce some latency, although this is likely to be minimal.

- **Processing overheads**: The data needs to be partitioned before being stored in an MPP-based data serving layer. Then, each node in the layer performs its processing. The processed data then needs to be consolidated. These additional steps create a processing overhead for small datasets.

- **Cost-effectiveness**: MPP can be cost-ineffective for smaller data volumes. Therefore, a minimal data volume threshold is expected to be reached before its performance advantages become evident. This threshold varies across different technologies. Typically, for a cloud-based MPP solution, this threshold is minimal.

Azure Synapse, **Teradata**, **Snowflake**, and **Amazon Redshift** are a few examples of MPP-based databases.

Now that we have learned about SQL-based data serving, let's discuss NoSQL-based data serving.

NoSQL-based serving

Data in the data serving layer is not just used for analytics. It can be used for serving data in real time or it can be exposed as an API. The SQL-based data serving layer that we discussed previously is not an ideal data serving layer for such requirements. **NoSQL** can also be used for such requirements. We will now briefly discuss some common types of NoSQL-based data serving solutions.

Document databases

Document databases are a type of NoSQL database that store data in documents like objects. **JSON** is the typical data structure used in document databases. In this instance, each record contains data as values of various types, including strings, numbers, Booleans, arrays, and objects. The document databases can scale when more documents are added to the database. Therefore, they can scale out and accommodate large volumes of data. Because of their flexibility and scalability, they are used in a variety of use cases.

Document databases are helpful when there is a requirement for a flexible schema. They provide fast queries, a structure well suited to handling big data, flexible indexing, and a simplified database method. In addition, document databases can be used as a data serving layer for providing real-time access to data. This pattern is widely used for downstream applications, such as mobile or web applications that demand minimal latency and frequent updates. Examples of these can be product or service catalogs, or applications that provide personalized experiences to end users.

MongoDB, **DocumentDB**, and **Cosmos DB** are a few examples of document databases.

Key-value stores

Key-value stores use associative arrays as their building blocks. Each item contains keys and values. As a result, key-value stores are better for use cases where you need to store large amounts of data. There is no need to perform complex queries but there's a requirement for low latency.

Many implementations of key-value stores (such as **Redis**) employ in-memory technology that makes them fast and effective for caching data. Examples of data stored in a cache could be precomputed values or a copy of data stored on a disk. Caching enables a decrease in data access latency, improves throughput, and eases the load on your relational database. Key-value stores are also used to implement the lightweight queueing systems frequently used in chat and messaging applications.

Key-value stores are predominantly used to manage session data for internet-scale applications. These kinds of databases can provide sub-second latency and are resilient in their design. With such characteristics, they are used for handling internet session data and any other low-latency applications.

Redis and **DynamoDB** are popular key-value stores.

Wide-column stores

Like relational databases, **wide-column stores** use tables, rows, and columns to store data. However, unlike in a relational database, the structure and content of the column can vary from row to row in the same table. As one can imagine, since the column formats can vary between rows in the same table, this offers certain benefits, such as the speed of querying, the scalability, and the flexibility of the data model. Wide-column stores excel in scenarios where there are many writes on the database compared to reads with no need to join data or aggregations.

Wide-column stores track **Internet of Things (IoT)** events and history, storing time-series data and transaction logging. **Apache Cassandra** and **HBase** are commonly used wide-column stores.

Data-sharing technology

The concept of **data sharing** is gaining traction in modern data analytics frameworks. As organizations store and curate more and more data, there is a need to share the data with internal and external stakeholders in a controlled and structured manner. In addition, organizations can also decide to **monetize** their data by sharing it with third parties and generating revenue from its usage. For organizations to realize these benefits, data-sharing technologies are used to share data in a controlled manner. The following figure depicts the process of data sharing. Data-sharing technology should be able to enable this workflow and facilitate data sharing in a controlled manner:

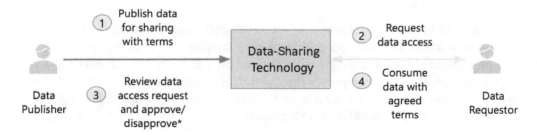

Figure 4.12 – A data-sharing workflow

The data-sharing workflow includes the following steps:

1. The data publisher publishes the data with the data-sharing technology. The data is published with its associated terms, charging mechanism, and conditions of usage.

2. A data requestor can browse through the data catalog and identify any data of interest. Once the data has been identified, a request to access or procure the data is sent.

3. An optional process in the workflow is to send the request to the data publisher. The data publisher can then approve or disapprove the request. This step is crucial when the data being shared is sensitive and the requestor needs to be vetted.

4. Once the data use has been approved by the publisher, the data is consumed by the data requestor. The data can then be used as per the terms of use.

Now, let's move on to cover the Summary of the chapter.

Summary

This chapter covered the details of how data is stored in the data lake and the data serving layer. In the first section, we covered how data is stored in the data lake layer. In the next section, we discussed the different types of datastores within the data lake and how they interact. We also delved into the different formats we can use to store data in a data lake and discussed the advantages and disadvantages of each of these formats.

In the next section, we focussed on the data serving layer. We explored SQL-based data serving stores, NoSQL-based serving stores, and the methods of data sharing. Finally, we examined the use cases and technologies for each of the different components in the data serving layer.

The next chapter will focus on data analytics, where we will cover the different types of analytics and the components used to derive insights from data.

Further reading

For more information regarding the topics that were covered in this chapter, take a look at the following resources:

- *HDFS Architecture Guide*: https://hadoop.apache.org/docs/r1.2.1/hdfs_design.html

- *Azure Data Lake Storage Gen2 Hierarchical Namespace | Microsoft Docs*: https://docs.microsoft.com/en-us/azure/storage/blobs/data-lake-storage-namespace

- *Comma-separated values*: https://en.wikipedia.org/wiki/Comma-separated_values
- *Parquet*: https://parquet.apache.org/documentation/latest/
- *JSON*: https://www.json.org/json-en.html
- *What is Parquet*: https://databricks.com/glossary/what-is-parquet
- *Architecture of Hbase*: https://www.geeksforgeeks.org/architecture-of-hbase/
- *Video File Formats*: https://www.computer.org/publications/tech-news/trends/8-best-video-file-formats-for-2020/
- *Redis*: https://redis.io/documentation
- *NoSQL Databases*: https://profil-software.com/blog/development/database-comparison-sql-vs-nosql-mysql-vs-postgresql-vs-redis-vs-mongodb/
- *Cassandra*: https://cassandra.apache.org/_/index.html
- *NoSQL Explained*: https://www.mongodb.com/nosql-explained

5
Deriving Insights from a Data Lakehouse

A lot of ground has been covered so far. The previous chapters covered the methods of ingesting, processing, storing, and serving data in a data lakehouse. Transforming the underlying data into insights is the core aim of any data analytics platform, so this chapter will focus on how to do this. We will also explore the different kinds of data analytics that can be employed in this process.

First, we'll discuss some of the business requirements relating to data analytics. Then, we'll explore different kinds of data analytics and how different stakeholders can use them. After that, we will dive into how these capabilities are enabled using the three components of the data analytics layer: the **analytics sandbox**, the **business intelligence service**, and the **artificial intelligence service**. We will cover different types of *descriptive* and *advanced* data analytics. We will also focus on the methods of enabling these analytics capabilities in a data lakehouse by considering the roles and processes involved.

We will cover the following topics in the chapter:

- Discussing the themes of analytics capabilities
- Enabling analytics capabilities in a data lakehouse

Discussing the themes of analytics capabilities

Data analytics is the process through which *data* is transformed into *insights*. Before getting into the technical components that enable this transformation, let's discuss themes of analytics capabilities that an organization requires. The analytical capabilities are targeted at two types of personas:

- **Technical users**: Technical users are stakeholders with the technical skills to directly engage with the underlying data structures. They have skills in SQL, programming, data science, and data engineering. A typical technical user could be a data analyst, data engineer, data scientist, or data architect.

- **Functional users**: Functional users are stakeholders with expertise in the specific functional domain, but their focus on technology is limited. They are subject matter experts, and they understand how the business or a particular domain functions. A typical functional user could be a business analyst or manager.

The following table summarizes the capabilities organizations require from data analytics, along with the stakeholders (personas) who would use them and the enablers who would implement them:

Analytics Capability Type	Analytics Capability	Capability Description	Stakeholder Type	Capability Enablers
Descriptive Analytics	On-demand Query	Capability to query underlying data on-demand for analysis.	Technical User	A platform that enables on-demand querying of data.
Descriptive Analytics	Standard Reporting	Capability to create standard reports for distribution.	Functional User	A platform that enables creation, scheduling, and distribution of reports.
Descriptive Analytics	Self-service Business Intelligence	Capability to enable end users to create their own analysis.	Functional User	Platform that can provide a GUI-based interface for data exploration or report creation.
Descriptive Analytics	Big Data Exploration	Capability to explore data for hypothesis generation.	Technical User	A platform that enables big data exploration.
Advanced Analytics	Machine Learning Model Development and Deployment	Capability to apply machine learning algorithms on data.	Technical User	A platform that enables experimentation and model deployment using machine learning algorithms, including deep learning algorithms.

Figure 5.1 – Data analytics capabilities

There are two types of data analytics provided by a data lakehouse:

- **Descriptive analytics**
- **Advanced analytics**

Let's explore each of these types in detail.

Descriptive analytics

Descriptive analytics takes the form of **on-demand queries, standard reporting, self-service business intelligence**, and **data lake exploration**. This category of analytics performs analytics on historical data by providing different points of view on the data. The points of view are created by aggregating and filtering the quantitative data (also called the *measure*), and slicing the data across attributes of functional dimensions, such as sales, customers, and products. We can deliver descriptive analytics in multiple formats such as files, cross tab reports, visual reports, or dashboards.

Let's now explore the types of descriptive analytics.

On-demand queries

The first data analytics capability required by any organization is to query the data in the data lake (or data warehouse) on demand. This is typically used to understand underlying data patterns, perform analysis, and get data for pointed functional queries.

For example, imagine that it is the fiscal year's last day, and the sales team needs to act fast to close the numbers. The sales department wants to know the list of customers who have yet to renew their loyalty programs. One last push to provide them with promos may help them meet or even exceed their targets. A technical analyst who is well-versed with the underlying data model of the data lake could create an ad hoc query using SQL and provide the answers.

The preceding example is just one use of on-demand queries. The functional questions can be many and can be ad hoc as well. Therefore, it may not be feasible to create pre-built reports to answer these queries. Instead, an analyst with the right technical skills can directly query the underlying database to provide instant answers.

Standard reporting

The second type of analytics that an organization could require is *standard reporting*. These reports provide the aggregated or granular measures that are pivoted across functional dimensions such as products, customers, and more. They are generated periodically based on specific functional requirements. They are then scheduled to be distributed to relevant stakeholders through multiple channels such as mobile apps, e-mail, and more. In addition, these standard reports provide a view of the current or historical state of business areas such as sales, marketing, and finance.

As the name indicates, *standard* reports are pre-defined. They are created by tapping into the data in the data serving layers and pre-defined reporting formats and elements. They are generally made by technical analysts and distributed to various non-technical functional users as required.

For example, imagine that a bank's compliance department needs to send a set of standard reports to the banking regulatory authorities every month. These reports have fixed formats, and the data elements of the reports rarely change. Therefore, a standard report created from the data warehouse can be generated and sent to the relevant stakeholders during the prescribed period.

Self-service business intelligence

The third type of analytics that an organization could require is *self-service business intelligence*. Self-service business intelligence provides functional users with a few technical skills to perform their analysis without relying on a technologist. Typically, self-service business intelligence offers a **Graphical User Interface** (**GUI**) that enables the functional users to slice and dice the data to derive actionable insights.

For example, imagine that a retail category manager wants to view the sales of the categories they manage across multiple stores in the country for the last month, as well as the top 10 products within each category. The category manager can use a self-service business intelligence platform to slice the sales data across the dimensions of products, stores, and the time period in order to get this view. In addition, the analysis that is created can be sliced and diced to create different views of the data.

This type of report is difficult to standardize, as different category managers may want to analyze the categories differently. Hence the need for self-service business intelligence to provide a frictionless platform for functional users to create their data insights.

Data lake exploration

The fourth type of data analytics that an organization could require is to explore its data lake. Data lake exploration is different from on-demand queries. As explained in *Chapter 4, Storing and Serving Data in a Data Lakehouse*, the data lake layers store structured and unstructured data. As it accumulates all kinds of data, it becomes a hotbed for deriving new insights and generating hypotheses. Therefore, the ability to explore data lakes efficiently becomes paramount for tapping into the rich data. As the data volumes are large and the formats are varied in data lakes, traditional SQL-based tools may not fully suffice when trying to derive insights.

Let's illustrate the requirement for data lake exploration with a scenario: imagine that a data scientist wants to build a targeted propensity model. To shortlist the features that can create a superior model, the data scientist needs to explore multiple features (columns) and then shortlist a feature set. Data lake exploration provides the ability to explore features and find the best features for a particular model.

Typically, a notebook-based interactive development environment combines features for code development, data visualization, and documentation for data lake exploration. **Jupyter Notebook** is one example of an open source tool that is used for data lake exploration.

Advanced analytics

Now that we have covered descriptive analytics, let's discuss **advanced analytics**. Advanced analytics pivots around machine learning methods. Machine learning employs statistical learning methods to perform analysis on data. These statistical methods utilize algorithms that predict what may happen based on historical data or extract complex mathematical relationships from data to generate insights.

The following figure illustrates the relationship between **artificial intelligence (AI)**, machine learning, and deep learning. Deep learning is a subset of machine learning, and machine learning is a subset of AI:

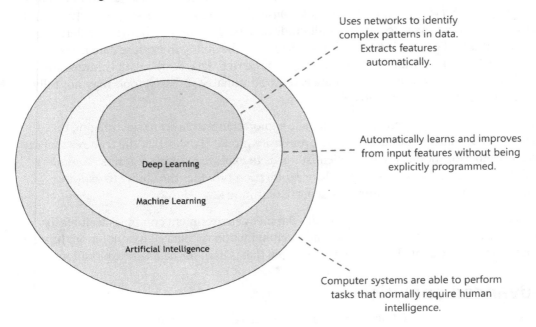

Figure 5.2 – The layers of advanced analytics

- A machine learning task is performed by creating a machine learning model. One or more algorithms combine to create the machine learning model. If the machine learning model uses a family of **artificial neural networks**, they are referred to as deep learning models.

- Machine learning is a deep topic in itself and covering it in depth is beyond the scope of this book. However, the following is a high-level view of two major categories of machine learning:

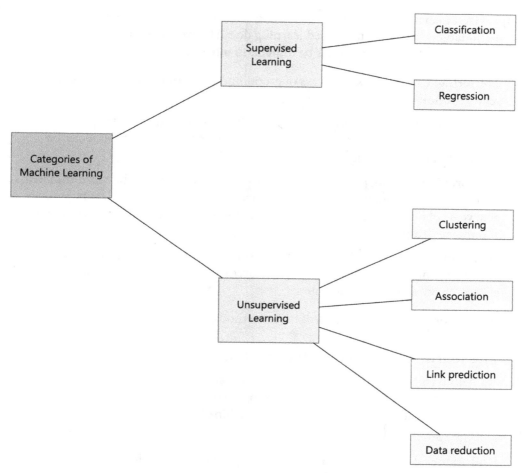

Figure 5.3 – Categories of machine learning

Supervised learning: Supervised learning is a type of machine learning task where there is a defined target. Conceptually, a modeler will supervise the machine learning model to achieve a particular goal. Supervised learning can be further classified into two types:

- **Regression**: Regression is the workhorse of machine learning tasks. It is used to estimate or predict numeric variables.

- **Classification**: As the name suggests, classification models classify something. It is estimated which bucket is best suited.

Unsupervised Learning: Unsupervised learning is a class of machine learning tasks where there are no targets. Since unsupervised learning doesn't have any specified target, the results they churn out may sometimes be difficult to interpret:

- **Clustering**: Clustering is a process of grouping similar things together. **Customer segmentation** uses clustering methods.

- **Association**: Association is a method of finding products that are frequently matched with each other. **Market basket analysis** in retail uses the association method to bundle products together.

- **Link prediction**: Link prediction is used to find the connection between data items. Recommendation engines employed by **Facebook**, **Amazon**, and **Netflix** make heavy use of link prediction algorithms to recommend as friends, items to purchase, and movies, respectively.

- **Data reduction**: Data reduction methods simplify the dataset from many features to a few features. They can take a large dataset with many attributes and find ways to express them with fewer attributes.

Let's focus on some specific examples of these methods.

Machine learning model development and deployment

Typically, before embarking on a machine learning task, a functional problem is defined, and that functional problem is broken down into one or more machine learning tasks. Once the machine learning task is defined, any machine learning model life cycle goes through five stages:

1. **Exploratory data analysis**: The first step is to explore the underlying data to identify the optimal features for model building.

2. **Data preparation**: The second step is creating the features that will be used as the input for the machine learning model. This process is also known as **feature engineering**.

3. **Model development**: The third step is developing the model by experimenting with various algorithms on a subset of historical data, choosing the best-fit algorithm for the model, and evaluating the model's performance. This process is known as **model training**.

4. **Model evaluation**: The fourth step is evaluating the model's performance on unseen data using machine learning performance metrics. This process is also known as **model testing**.

5. **Model deployment**: Finally, the fifth step is to **deploy** the usage model for consumption.

The advanced analytics capability of data lakes should provide the tools required to progress through the five stages of the model development life cycle. Typically, deep learning models excel when using unstructured data such as images, audio, text, and more. Deep learning models require much more computing power to train the model. Therefore, the required capability is not just limited to the standard machine learning algorithms, such as **decision trees** and **Support-Vector Machines (SVMs)**, but also encompasses deep learning algorithms such as **Convolutional Neural Networks (CNNs)**, **Recurrent Neural Networks (RNNs)**, and more.

Now that we have covered some of the different types of analytics, let's discuss the ways to enable these capabilities in a data lakehouse.

Enabling analytics capabilities in a data lakehouse

The previous section defined the different types of analytics that need to be fulfilled by a data lakehouse. Now, let's focus on how a data lakehouse enables these capabilities. Recall that in *Chapter 2, The Data Lakehouse Architecture Overview*, we defined the logical architecture of a data lakehouse. One of the layers of the architecture was the data analytics layer, which interacts with the data lake layer and the data serving layer. The following figure illustrates this interaction between the layers of the data lakehouse architecture:

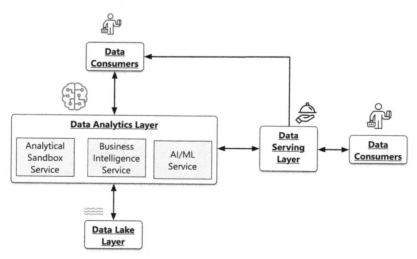

Figure 5.4 – The interaction between the data lakehouse layers

The three components of the data analytics layer are as follows:

- Analytical sandbox service
- Business intelligence service
- AI/ML service

The following figure maps the required analytics capabilities to the components that fulfill them:

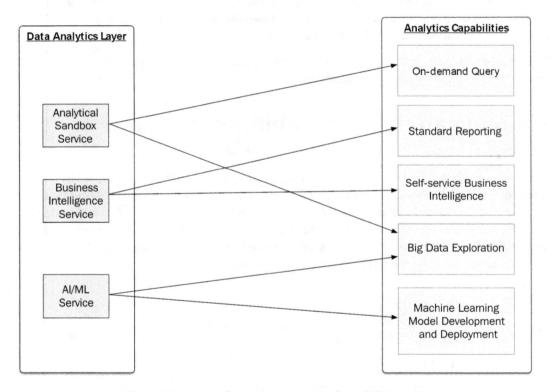

Figure 5.5 – An analytics components and capabilities map

Now, let's see how each of these services works.

The analytics sandbox service

Analytics is also about data exploration. With large volumes of data stored in the data lake and the data warehouses, it becomes essential to play with data, perform ad hoc analysis, and create hypotheses that can be proved or disproved. An analytics sandbox enables this. An analytics sandbox enables two analytics capabilities:

1. First, it allows on-demand querying of the data lake or the data warehouse.
2. Second, it allows big data exploration.

The following figure shows that analytics sandboxes enable technical users such as data scientists and analysts to explore and query data lakes and data warehouses:

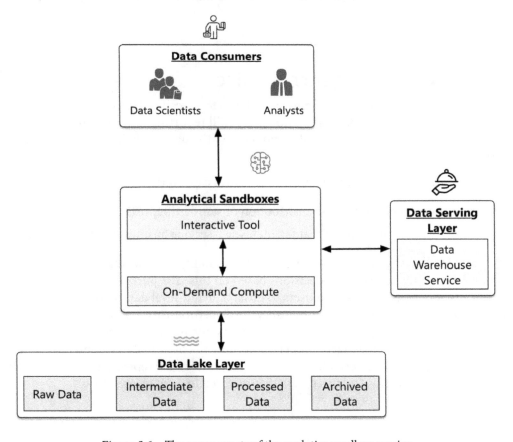

Figure 5.6 – The components of the analytics sandbox service

An analytics sandbox can instantiate an on-demand compute cluster that interacts with the data lake and the data warehouse. Depending on the type of analysis that needs to be performed, the compute cluster can be varied. An on-demand **Spark** cluster or SQL cluster are examples of such sandboxes. The interaction between the analytics sandbox and the data lake/data warehouse is facilitated by an **interaction tool**.

Interactive notebook services such as Jupyter Notebook and **Apache Zeppelin** – popular open source projects that enable analysis using interactive notebooks – are good examples of interaction tools. Interactive notebooks or **integrated development environments (IDEs)** can provide a platform for analysis using programming languages such as **R**, **Python**, **Scala**, **SQL**, and more. These interactive notebooks or IDEs provide interactive computational environments that combine code execution, rich text, mathematics, plots, and rich media.

Let's now cover the business intelligence service.

The business intelligence service

Business intelligence has been the staple for analytics for decades. However, today, organizations need a robust analytics platform to fulfill reporting requirements. The business intelligence service is a crucial component of the data analytics layer that meets these requirements.

The business intelligence service enables two analytics capabilities:

1. First, it allows the creation and distribution of standard reports.
2. Second, it enables a platform that facilitates self-service business intelligence.

The business intelligence goal should be to enable the ability to view, analyze, and understand data, and make critical decisions based on this. The purpose of business intelligence reporting is to allow end users to observe detail-level data so that it can be analyzed and understood, thereby giving users the ability to turn data into actionable information. The following figure shows that business intelligence services enable functional users – such as management personnel and business analysts – and reporting systems to connect to the underlying data serving layer to create reports. Typically, report creation requires clean and structured data that is stored in a data warehouse.

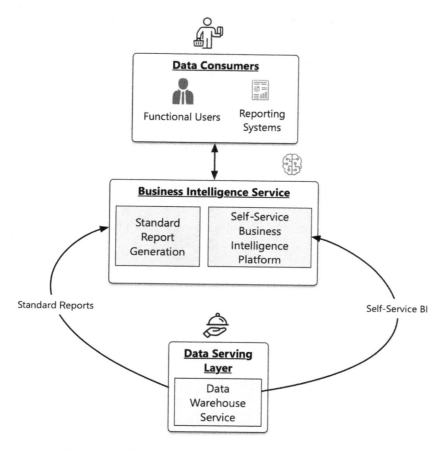

Figure 5.7 – The components of the business intelligence service

The business intelligence service enables the generation of standard reports. Standard reports can take multiple forms, which may range from a set of canned reports to visual dashboards. Canned reports have a pre-defined structure. They are scheduled periodically to be delivered to target stakeholders. On the other hand, visual dashboards aggregate data. They attempt to show data patterns and relationships using charts and other visual aids. The goal here is to distill data into insights to guide actions. The other part of the business intelligence service is the ability to create self-service analysis by the functional user who can slice and dice data as required.

Self-service business intelligence platforms enable **Online Analytical Processing (OLAP)** that can create user-friendly depictions of data in the form of measures and dimensions. A functional user with no technical knowledge can drag and drop these measures and dimensions to develop an analysis in a report, chart, or even dashboard to aid their decision-making processes. This process requires no intervention by technical users.

Microsoft Power BI, **Tableau**, and **Qlik** are popular business intelligence tools that enable standard reporting and self-service business intelligence.

Let's move on to AI services next.

The AI service

The last analytics service that is fulfilled by the data analytics layer is the AI service. The critical analytics capabilities that this service enables are as follows:

1. First, it allows big data exploration.
2. Second, it facilitates the development and deployment of machine learning models.

The following figure shows the interactions between various layers of a data lakehouse and the AI service:

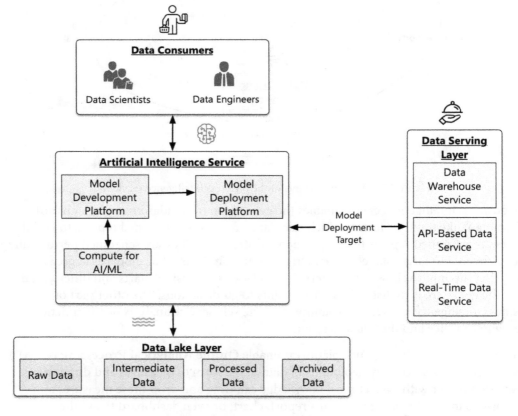

Figure 5.8 – The components of the AI service

Two significant stakeholders interact with this service:

- **Data scientists**: Data scientists perform the following essential tasks:

  - First, they explore the data that is available for model building.

  - Second, they create new features through feature engineering to incorporate the features in a model.

  - Third, they develop and test models by experimenting with various machine learning algorithms.

  - Finally, they monitor model performance over time and tweak models as required to maintain metrics.

- **Data engineers**: Data engineers perform the following essential tasks:

  - They create various data pipelines to create the input data for model development.

  - They deploy machine learning models periodically with live data and ensure that the correct model versions are deployed and updated continually.

The AI service interacts with both the data serving layer and the data lake layer. As with the analytics sandbox service, an on-demand compute instance is attached to the model creation platform. This compute instance provides the computing resources to perform the required exploratory data analysis, feature engineering, model training, and model testing. The compute instance can also be based on **graphics processing units** (**GPU**), which are extensively used to train deep learning models.

One type of model development platform is a GUI-based platform. Such platforms provide visual model development capabilities – that is, an interface that offers pre-built machine learning modules such as data preparation, cleaning, statistical analysis, and algorithms, which can be weaved together in a workflow for model generation. **Azure Machine Learning** is one such cloud-based service that provides a GUI for model development. The other type of model development platform can be based on programming languages. Almost all major programming languages have packages and modules for machine learning; for example, Python and R are top programming languages that specialize in machine learning. Deep learning frameworks that use artificial neural networks for machine learning can also be based on Python. **TensorFlow**, **PyTorch**, and **Apache MXNet** are popular deep learning frameworks.

This section covered the ways in which three major data analytics capabilities can be enabled in a data lakehouse. Now, let's summarize the chapter.

Summary

This chapter covered the data analytics layer, which is a vital element in a data lakehouse. We explained that transforming data into insights is the core aim of any data analytics platform, and we looked at how this can be achieved in detail.

We started by exploring some of the different business requirements of data analytics. Then, we covered different users and how they interact with data analytics. We showed how descriptive and advanced analytics form the broad categories of analytics that organizations typically require. We then discussed the characteristics of these categories in detail. Next, we drilled down into different analytics capabilities within these categories. After that, we discussed five analytics capabilities that are important for fulfilling the analytical needs of an organization.

We then mapped the three components of the data analytics layer with their analytics capabilities. Finally, the chapter discussed the sub-components required in each of the three components and how they interact with other layers of the data lakehouse architecture to facilitate analytics.

The next chapter will focus on how data governance is used to explore data in a data lakehouse.

Further reading

For more information regarding the topics that were covered in this chapter, take a look at the following resources:

- *Jupyter*: `https://jupyter.org/`
- *Machine Learning*: `https://en.wikipedia.org/wiki/Machine_learning`
- *Data Science Process*: `https://becominghuman.ai/data-science-simplified-principles-and-process-b06304d63308`
- *Deep Learning*: `https://rpradeepmenon.medium.com/an-executive-primer-to-deep-learning-80c1ece69b34`
- *Zeppelin*: `https://zeppelin.apache.org/`
- *BI Reporting*: `https://www.jinfonet.com/resources/bi-defined/bi-reporting/`
- *What is Business Intelligence?* `https://www.cio.com/article/2439504/business-intelligence-definition-and-solutions.html`

- *Power B*: https://powerbi.microsoft.com/en-us/

- *Qlik*: https://www.qlik.com/us/

- *Tableau*: https://www.tableau.com/trial/tableau-online

- *Azure Machine Learning*: https://azure.microsoft.com/en-us/services/machine-learning/

- *Python*: https://www.python.org/

- *R*: https://www.r-project.org/

- *Pytorch*: https://pytorch.org/

- *TensorFlow*: https://www.tensorflow.org/

- *MXNET*: https://mxnet.apache.org/versions/1.8.0/

- *GPU Acceleration*: https://www.nvidia.com/en-sg/deep-learning-ai/solutions/data-science/

6
Applying Data Governance in the Data Lakehouse

The journey so far has covered five layers of Data Lakehouse. This chapter will focus on the final two layers, that is, data governance and data security layers. Data governance and security is an essential aspect of the modern data analytics platform. We will start this chapter by discussing the need for a data governance framework and how the 3-3-3 framework outlines the three components of data governance. The next section of the chapter will discuss implementing the data governance components in the Data Lakehouse. The sections will first cover implementing the three data governance components. Then, the sections will include key constructs for each of the data governance components and practical methods to implement them.

We will cover the following topics in the chapter:

- The 3-3-3 framework for data governance
- The three components of data governance

The 3-3-3 framework for data governance

The data landscape of any organization changes rapidly as more and more organizations embark on the digital transformation journey, and more and more data footprints are created.

Efficiently collecting, managing, and harnessing this data footprint is pivotal for an organization's success. Therefore, data needs to be treated as a strategic asset. However, according to a survey conducted by *McKinsey in 2019, on average, an employee spends around 29 percent of the time on non-value-added tasks due to poor data quality and availability*. The lack of quality of data and the lack of proper data availability is a function of data governance. As more and more data becomes available for analysis, the principle of *garbage in, garbage out* begins to manifest.

The 3-3-3 framework creates a structure that is a great starting point:

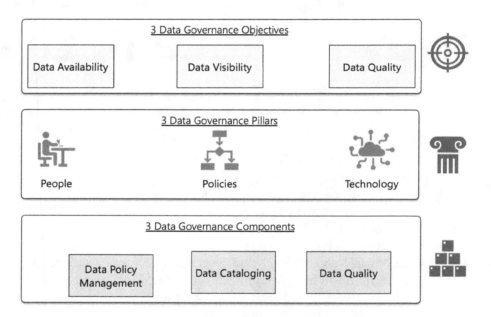

Figure 6.1 – 3-3-3 framework for data governance

This framework focuses on the following three aspects:

- **Objectives**
- **Pillars**
- **Components**

Let's discuss each of these aspects in detail.

The three objectives of data governance

Holistic data governance starts with a well-defined vision and clear objectives that define what data governance should achieve. The goals of data governance are specific to the organization. In this chapter, we will discuss only three objectives that are common and a must-have for any organization. The three **must-have** data governance objectives are as follows:

1. **Data Availability**: Data availability ensures that a platform is provided to the right stakeholders for finding the correct data on time.

2. **Data Visibility**: Data visibility ensures an intuitive catalog of data assets available across the organization.

3. **Data Quality**: Data quality ensures that the appropriate quality of data is maintained throughout the data life cycle.

The three pillars of data governance

Now that we have defined the objectives, let's now discuss the three pillars of data governance.

People

The first pillar of data governance is the *people*. People embody personnel who perform three tasks:

*   **Creating**: Ensuring that proper data governance policies are created, periodically reviewed, and updated as required. You should create these policies based on the strategic vision that the organization has for its data.

*   **Monitoring**: Ensuring that the organization uses the data under the policy that has been created.

*   **Maintaining**: Ensuring that proper processes are implemented to maintain data quality and make data accessible within and outside the organization.

Many roles fulfill these three tasks, and their responsibilities may vary from organization to organization. However, the following table represents the key roles that are generally required in any data governance framework:

Role	Key Responsibility
Executive Sponsor	This role has the authority and budget and is accountable for ensuring data governance is established.
Data Governance Lead	This role has the overall accountability and responsibility for implementing the data governance program.
Data Owners	This role comes with authority and budget for overseeing the quality and protection of a specific data subject area. The role also decides who has the right to access and maintain that data and its usage.
Data Steward	This role is responsible for overseeing the quality and protection of a specific data area. This role is typically an expert in a specific data domain and works with other data stewards across the enterprise. In addition, the role ensures that the data quality is maintained.
Data Publishing Manager	This role is responsible for quality assurance, checking, and publishing newly created trusted data assets for consumers to find and use in a data marketplace.

Figure 6.2 – Key roles for data governance

Now, let's discuss the second pillar of data governance, that is, policy.

Creating data policy

The second pillar of data governance is policy. The data goes through many stages of the life cycle throughout its journey in the Data Lakehouse. For each data life cycle stage, specific rules need to be defined that cater to data discovery, usage, and monitoring. The following figure depicts stages of the data life cycle and the implementation of policies:

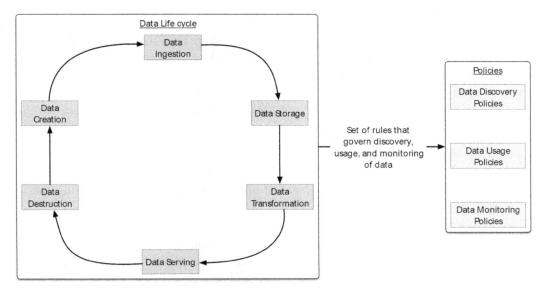

Figure 6.3 – Stages of the data life cycle and implementation of policies

The three categories of policies applied across the data life cycle are as follows:

- **Data Discovery Policies**: The data discovery policies are a set of rules that cater to the process of data discovery, profiling, and cataloging. These policies may vary based on the organization. These policies dictate how the data in the Data Lakehouse is cataloged and discovered.

- **Data Usage Policies**: The data usage policies are a set of rules that cater to data usage in the Data Lakehouse. It spans across the entire life cycle of the data and clarifies three key aspects:

  - First, who can see the data?

  - Second, how is the data transformed during its entire life cycle?

  - Third, how is the data supposed to be used?

- **Data Monitoring Policies**: The data monitoring policies are rules that cater to the monitoring and auditing of data. These policies create a view of the data usage activities, data quality, and how data is maintained and retained. This set of rules also outlines how any policy violation is detected, documented, and resolved.

Now, let's discuss the third pillar of data governance, that is, technology.

Technology

The third pillar of data governance is technology. Technology is an integral part of any data governance framework. Technology implies the product or service that is used for performing the aspects of data governance. The three components of data governance come to fruition by appropriate use of technologies. A plethora of technologies can be used to implement data governance. However, the technology choice should enable the following at the minimum:

1. **Enables implementation of policy workflow**: As discussed in the previous sections, data governance is policy-driven. Therefore, these policies need to be implemented using a technology that allows the creation of policies and provides a workflow for proper policy management.

2. **Enables implementation of data cataloging**: The technology used should perform data cataloging of multiple data assets across the organization's data ecosystem. It should also be able to facilitate the easy discovery of the data through intuitive search. The data cataloging tool should also be able to classify the data and provide insights on data usage.

3. **Enables implementation of data quality**: The technology used should be able to check the data quality aspects of the data. In addition, it should be able to configure *data quality rules* and ensure that you can create a data quality map across multiple data quality dimensions.

Let's now move on to the three components of the data governance layer.

The three components of the data governance layer

Recall that in *Chapter 2, Data Lakehouse Architecture Overview*, we briefly discussed the three components of the data governance layer. The following figure provides a recap of the three components of data governance:

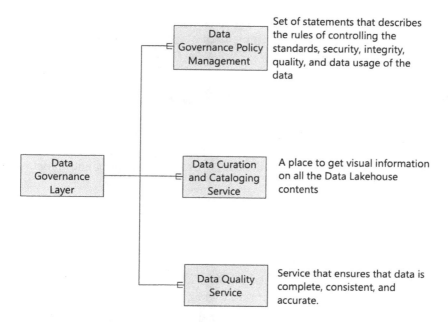

Figure 6.4 – The three components of the data governance layer

The three components of data governance are as follows:

- **Data Governance Policy Management**: The first component is not a technology component; it is a set of data policies and standards. The data policy is a set of statements describing the rules of controlling the standards, security, integrity, quality, and data usage in the Data Lakehouse.

- **Data Curation and Cataloging Service**: Data cataloging is the process of organizing an inventory of data so that it can be easily identified. This service ensures that all the source data, the data in the data lake, the data in the data warehouse, the data processing pipelines, and the outputs extracted from the Data Lakehouse are appropriately cataloged. Think of data cataloging services as the Facebook of data – a place to get visual information on all the Data Lakehouse's contents, including information about the relationships between the data and the lineage of transformations that the data has gone through. This service also provides insights about the metadata in the form of dashboards or reports.

- **Data Quality Service**: Any data stored or ingested in the Data Lakehouse must have a data quality score that determines the reliability and usability of the data. There are many parameters on which the quality of data is determined. A few of these parameters include the completeness of data, the consistency of data, and the accuracy of the data. The data quality service ensures that data is complete, consistent, and accurate.

Now that we have clarified the 3-3-3 framework for data governance, let's deep-dive into how you can use this framework to implement holistic data governance for the Data Lakehouse.

Implementing data governance policy management

The implementation of data governance policy management goes through two stages, which are as follows:

1. The first stage is to define *what* the data policy is and the components of data policies.

2. The last stage is to answer *how* the data policies are implemented.

Let's explore each of these stages in detail:

Defining data governance policy

A data governance policy is a documented set of guidelines that ensures that an organization's data and information assets are managed consistently and used correctly. The data components of a data governance policy include the following:

- **Charter**: A data governance charter is a statement of intent for the organization to follow as it designs and implements its data governance program. This charter defines the over-management of data availability, usability, integrity, and security. It establishes the parameters around data, so there is consistency in how it is published and how consumers use it.

- **Tenets**: Tenets are a set of *architectural principles* focused on ingestion, storage, processing, serving, and securing the data. The tenets may differ based on the organization's maturity and its vision. A few examples of tenets are as follows:

    - Have purpose-driven storage layers – a data lake to store all raw and interim data and serve data stores.

    - There will be decoupling between the storage of data and the compute required to process the data.

    - Use a **Platform as a Service (PaaS)** offering to leverage demand scalability, built-in **High Availability (HA)**, and minimal maintenance.

    - Architect in a modular manner. While architecting, focus on the functionality rather than on the technology.

    - All data and its transformation lineage needs to be captured in the Data Lakehouse.

Let's now discuss how organizations can realize data governance policies.

Realizing data governance policy

This stage covers the process of implementing and monitoring the data governance policies that are defined. The data governance policies are not cast in stone. It is a continuous cycle, and they need to be tweaked as the organization evolves and new information comes to light. The following figure depicts the continuous process of realizing the data governance policy:

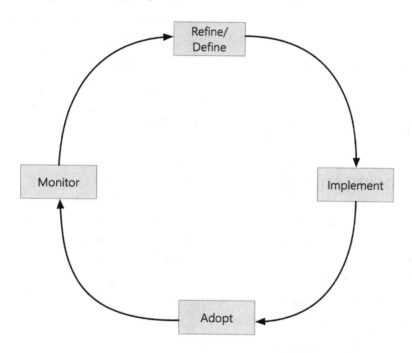

Figure 6.5 – A cycle to realize data governance

Let's zoom into each of the stages of the cycle.

1. **Refine/Define**: In the refine/define stage for realizing the data governance policy, the goal is to determine the policies suited to the organization. Typically, a **data governance committee** has representation from all the critical stakeholders and the roles depicted in the preceding section will be part of the committee. They will define the policies and refine them as they go through different stages of the life cycle.

2. **Implement**: In the implementation stage for realizing the data governance policy, a project or program is initiated to roll out the data governance policy across different functions of the organizations. The program team members, delivery methodology, and program milestones are crafted in this stage. Technical tools that you will employ to realize these policies are also identified.

3. **Adopt**: Adoption of the data governance process is essential. Without the right adoption, the prudent realization of data governance policy is not possible. Furthermore, once the program has been rolled out, the various stakeholders who need to be aware of the usage process should be trained and enabled. Finally, focusing on adoption ensures that the organization is aware of the benefits of data governance and how it helps drive towards a more data-driven organization.

4. **Monitor**: The last stage of the cycle is to monitor the adoption of data governance policy. This stage aims to identify which policies are effective and which ones are ineffective. The ineffective policies need to be revisited and refined to be more helpful.

Now that we have explored how to implement the data governance policy component, let's implement the data catalog component.

Implementing the data catalog

As described in *Chapter 2, The Data Lakehouse Architecture Overview*, data cataloging and curation is the process of organizing an inventory of data so that it can be easily identified. Data cataloging ensures that all the source system data, data in the data lake, the data warehouse, the data processing pipelines, and the outputs extracted from the Data Lakehouse are appropriately cataloged.

For implementing the data catalog, we will follow a similar thought process to implementing the data governance policies:

1. First, we will identify the guidelines for determining the elements to be cataloged. These elements define *what* needs to be cataloged.

2. Next, we will focus on *how* to implement the data catalog.

Let's cover the elements of cataloging next.

The elements of cataloging

The elements of cataloging can be explained using a catalog map. This provides potential metadata that can be cataloged. The following diagram provides a view of the catalog map, describing the minimum elements that need to be cataloged:

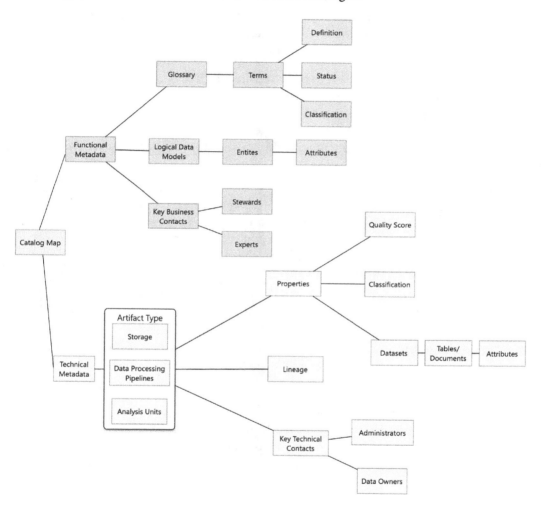

Figure 6.6 – Elements of the catalog map

The two types of metadata that need to be cataloged include **Functional** and **Technical**. Let's briefly describe each type of metadata.

- **Functional Metadata**: As the name suggests, functional metadata captures the metadata from a functional perspective and is technology agnostic. Functional metadata is an essential piece of cataloging as functional definitions change based on the view of an organizational unit. The key elements that need to be cataloged from a functional perspective are as follows:

  - **Glossary**: A glossary is meant to be the de facto source of commonly used terms that stakeholders across the organization can assess. A glossary captures terms, definitions of the term under different contexts, and its status within the cataloging function, that is, whether the term is in *review*, *approved*, or a *new entrant*. The glossary also documents the classification of a term, such as whether the term is personal information.

  - **Logical Data Models**: A logical data model is a blueprint that provides a functional view of the organization divided into subject areas, entities, and relationships between entities. The logical data models are helpful to get a high-level view of different entities in an organization, such as a customer in any industry. The logical data model should be cataloged. It enables the users to search for such blueprints and understand the various cogs that are elemental to the organization.

  - **Key Business Contacts**: Each business term in the glossary needs an *owner* who owns the definition of the term in the organization's context. These owners are called **Stewards**. Typically, these owners are assigned to each functional area and the one multiple term within that functional area. In addition, the key business contacts may also include **Experts** who are **Subject Matter Experts** (**SMEs**) in a particular functional area.

- **Technical Metadata**: As the name suggests, technical metadata captures the metadata from a technical perspective. It is particular to the technical components of the Data Lakehouse, such as storage files, databases, or transformation pipelines. The key elements that need to be cataloged from a technical perspective are as follows:

- **Artifact Type**: The artifact type signifies the types of technical artifacts that need to be cataloged. It can be a database, different types of data processing pipelines, or a unit of analysis, such as a report or a machine learning model. The source can be a structured or unstructured data source that can reside outside or within the purview of the Data Lakehouse. Within the ambit of the Data Lakehouse, the components in the data lake layer, the data-serving layer, the processing layer, and the analytics layer need to be cataloged.

- **Properties:** Each cataloged source has a set of properties that vary depending on the source type. For example, suppose it is a database. In that case, you can catalog information about the database type, the physical tables within it, and the columns for each table. Another example could be a data pipeline. Properties of the data pipelines include the source information, the data transformation information, and the target of the data pipeline. Properties can also have the **Quality Score** of a specific table or column. For example, if the data is in the raw data store of the data lake, it may be cleaned or filtered. As a result, such datasets will have a low quality score. On the other hand, if the data is in the serving layer, it will have been cleansed, filtered, and made ready for consumption. Hence its relative quality score will be higher.

- **Lineage**: The data cataloging should be able to support data lineage. Data lineage provides a view of how data has been transformed from the source to the analysis unit, such as a report. It gives an idea of the data journey.

- **Key Technical Contacts**: Like the key business contacts, each piece of technical metadata also has an *owner*. This owner can be the source system owner or a database administrator. The key contacts also include **Experts** who can provide insights into how data units are used and transformed.

Let's now discuss the process of implementing the data catalog.

The process of implementing the data catalog

The following figure illustrates the process of implementing the data catalog. It depicts the subcomponents of a data catalog service and its interaction with other components of the Data Lakehouse. Let's look into them in detail:

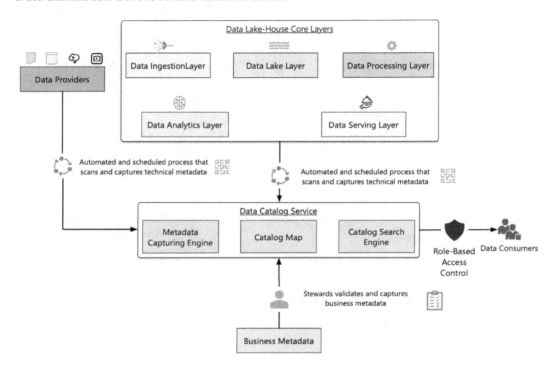

Figure 6.7 – The process of implementing the data catalog

The data cataloging process performs three steps to enable the catalog to be used for discovery. The steps are as follows:

1. **Metadata Capturing Engine**: The metadata capturing engine is the first component. It captures metadata through either data scanning or a manual process. Typically, a data scan process scans technical metadata from both the data providers, that is, data sources of the Data Lakehouse and the layers of the Data Lakehouse, that is, the data lake layer, the data serving layer, and so on. Data scanning is an automated process that taps into components such as databases and data pipelines to capture the metadata they provide. The method of scanning can be periodically scheduled so that any metadata changes can be automatically cataloged. The metadata information is captured, processed, and converted into a **Catalog Map**. Along with this technical metadata, the data steward also catalogs business metadata.

2. **Catalog Map**: The data scan *results* in a **Catalog Map**. The catalog map provides a map of metadata that the data consumers can browse to discover data elements that may be of interest to them. The catalog map enables the data consumers to explore the properties of data, such as its definition, lineage, and quality score. The catalog map can also have other features, such as providing *insights* about the data that is cataloged. For example, the catalog map may provide a report showing *how many cataloged attributes have sensitive information*. Once the catalog map is created, it is then exposed to the data consumers through the component of the **Catalog Search Engine**.

3. **Catalog Search Engine**: The **Catalog Search Engine** is the window to the catalog. It is the component through which the data consumers interact with the catalog. It provides the ability to search artifacts that are cataloged using keywords, concepts, and artifact types, and so on. Proper **Role-Based Access Control** (RBAC) is employed to ensure that access to the data catalog is restricted and allowed to only the data consumer who needs it.

Now that we have covered how to elaborate on the data catalog component, let's implement the data quality component.

Implementing data quality

As in any other analytics platform, data quality plays an important role even in the Data Lakehouse. The *garbage in, garbage out* philosophy is applicable. For a practical implementation of data quality in the Data Lakehouse, the first step is to create a data quality framework. The next step entails implementing the framework that you can apply to data in the Data Lakehouse. This framework then needs to be adopted and monitored continuously. Let's look into these steps in detail.

The data quality framework

Before creating the data quality framework, it is essential to define data quality. The data quality rules are applicable for any data stored in the Data Lakehouse, that is, in the data lake and serving layers.

Quality of data is defined as the ability of the data to be fit for practical usage.

The data in the Data Lakehouse will have many levels of quality. However, it is impractical to always have data of the utmost quality. As more and more processing and rules are applied to improve data quality, the cost of achieving that quality goes up. There is an inflection point somewhere, and the cost of achieving quality no longer justifies the value it brings in. Hence, there needs to be a balance in achieving data quality. The following figure shows the cyclical stages of a *data quality framework*. Let's explore each of these stages in detail:

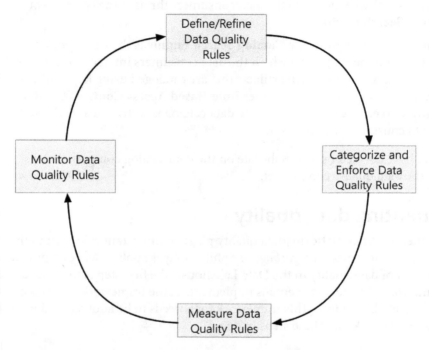

Figure 6.8 – The process of implementing the data catalog

Let's discuss how the data quality rules are defined and refined.

Defining/refining data quality rules

The first stage is to define the data quality rules and provide guidance on the potential methods of tackling aberrations of these rules. As shown in the following figure, you can define data quality rules at three levels:

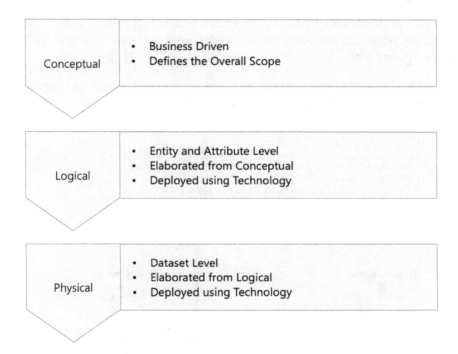

Figure 6.9 – The levels of data quality rules

Let's discuss each of these levels in detail.

- **Conceptual**: Defining data quality rules at a conceptual level involves providing a high-level data quality requirement. As a general guideline, data quality rules should be developed for the data elements showing the following characteristics:

  - A data element is visual to the functional unit.

  - A data element forms part of a functional key performance indicator.

  - A data element is part of a functional rule.

  - A data element is a user input in the application.

- **Logical**: Defining data quality rules at a logical level involves decomposing the conceptual-level data quality requirements into rules defined at a logical level. Each conceptual-data quality rule requirement can be split into one logical validation that you would eventually apply in a physical data object.

- **Physical**: Defining data quality rules at a physical level involves decomposing the data quality requirements defined at the logical level into data quality rules defined in a data quality tool.

For a better understanding of this concept, let's take an example of defining the data quality rule for a *manufacturing plant*:

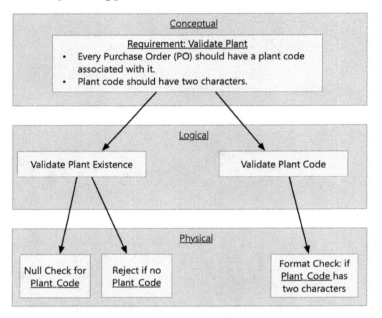

Figure 6.10 – An example of implementing data quality rules

Let's now discuss how to enforce the data quality rules.

Enforcing data quality rules

The second stage is to enforce the data quality rules as defined in *step 1*. Again, there are different dimensions through which you can enforce the data quality rules. The six dimensions are as follows:

- **Completeness**: Completeness of data implies the extent to which the required data has been recorded. A prudent data quality rule checks the completeness of data.

- **Timeliness**: Timeliness measures how frequently the recorded value is updated and verified to reflect the current value. Timeliness enforces keeping data current. Timeliness also includes accessibility, being able to gain access to the correct data when needed. The data quality rule should check the timeliness of data.

- **Uniqueness**: Uniqueness implies the presence of duplicate values of data emanating from multiple sources. The data quality rule should check the uniqueness of data.

- **Consistency**: Consistency implies the degree to which a data element contains the same types of information from record to record, based on its definition. The data quality rule should check for data consistency.

- **Validity**: The validity implies the degree to which the description of the data element and its business rules are appropriate and of high quality. The data quality rule should check for data validity.

- **Accuracy**: The accuracy of a data element implies the degree to which the data value reflects reality in conforming to the standard definition and business rules related to the creation, maintenance, and use of the data.

Measuring data quality rules

The third stage measures how the data is performing against the laid-out dimensions of data quality rules. Some frequently used metrics for measuring the quality score include the following:

- **Completeness score**: This is a measurement of how complete the data element is. An example of measuring the completeness score for a table can be the following: *count of relevant records / count of relevant records + count of missing records*.

- **Accuracy score**: The accuracy score is a measurement of how accurate the data element is. An example of measuring the accuracy score for a table can be the following: *count of relevant records – count of erroneous records / count of relevant records*.

- **Timeliness score**: A measurement of how timely or stale the data is. This measurement depends on the non-functional requirements and how much staleness is acceptable in a specific dataset.

- **Overall quality score**: The overall quality score is a weighted average of completeness, accuracy, and timeliness.

Monitoring data quality rules

The last stage of the cycle is to monitor the outcome of the data quality rules and their impact on the organization's data element. In practice, achieving a perfect overall quality score is extremely difficult. However, an organization should strive to estimate the overall quality score for each data element and continuously improve it to reach the goal. The data quality rules need to be constantly redefined to better the overall quality score.

Summary

We have covered a lot of ground in this chapter. The data governance layer, one of the vital layers in the Data Lakehouse, was covered in depth. We started by emphasizing the importance of data governance. The 3-3-3 framework for data governance provides a holistic framework for looking into data governance in a structured manner. As part of the 3-3-3 framework, *must-have* objectives for data governance were covered. The section also covered the key roles that enable data governance and the critical aspects of data governance policies, and the characteristics of technologies that allow it.

The next section of the chapter focused on the three components of the data governance layer, that is, data governance policy management, the data cataloging service, and the data quality service. The section then drilled down into *what* each component means and *how* the parts come to fruition in the Data Lakehouse architecture.

The next chapter will focus on the final layer of the Data Lakehouse, that is, the **Data Security Layer**.

Further reading

- *Data governance: The best practices framework for managing data assets (cio. com)*: `https://www.cio.com/article/202183/what-is-data-governance-a-best-practices-framework-for-managing-data-assets.html`

- *Designing data governance that delivers value | McKinsey*: `https://www.mckinsey.com/business-functions/mckinsey-digital/our-insights/designing-data-governance-that-delivers-value`

- *The TOGAF Standard, Version 9.2 - Architecture Governance (opengroup.org)*: `https://pubs.opengroup.org/architecture/togaf9-doc/arch/chap44.html`

- *Data Quality Dimensions*: `https://www.precisely.com/blog/data-quality/data-quality-dimensions-measure`

- *Data Quality Dimensions*: `https://www.collibra.com/blog/the-6-dimensions-of-data-quality`

7

Applying Data Security in a Data Lakehouse

Six layers of the data lakehouse have been covered so far. This chapter will cover the last layer of **Data Security**. It is the most crucial layer that ensures that data is secured in all the layers of a data lakehouse; this chapter will cover *the ways to secure* the data lakehouse. We will start by formulating a framework for data security, which will elucidate the key dimensions you need to consider for data security. The next section of the chapter will focus on three components of the data security layer that help secure the lake and provide the right access.

In summary, this chapter will cover the following:

- Realizing the data security components in a data lakehouse
- Using an identity and access management service in a data lakehouse
- Methods of data encryption in a data lakehouse
- Methods of data masking in a data lakehouse
- Methods of implementing network security in a data lakehouse

Let's begin by discussing the methods for realizing the data security components in a data lakehouse.

Realizing the data security components in a data lakehouse

We covered the elements of data security briefly in *Chapter 2, The Data Lakehouse Architecture Overview*. Recall that, in that chapter, we discussed the four key components of the data security layer. The following figure summarizes the four components of the data security layer:

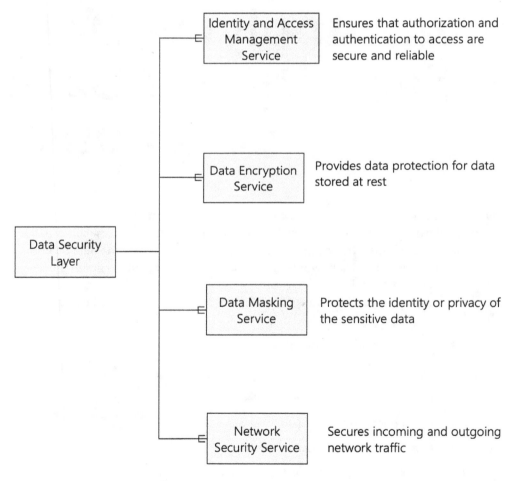

Figure 7.1 – Data security components

These four components ensure that data is well secured and that access to data is controlled. They work together in securing the data lakehouse. The following figure depicts how these four components orchestrate protected data:

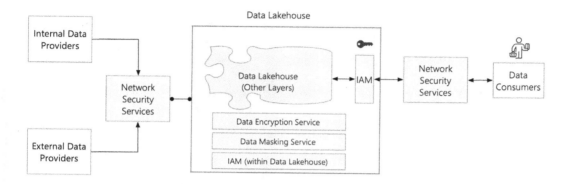

Figure 7.2 – Orchestration of various data security components in the data lakehouse

Whenever any interaction needs to be done with the data lakehouse layers, it must go through the **network security service**. The network security service filters the traffic to the data lakehouse layer. The network traffic to and from the data lakehouse layer is encrypted within the data lakehouse, using the **data encryption service**; specific sensitive data is masked using the **data masking service**. The **Identity and Access Management (IAM)** service ensures that **Role-Based Access Control (RBAC)** is applied. With RBAC, access to the data lakehouse components is provided with the right level of authentication and authorization.

Now that we have covered the overall flow, let's discuss each of these components in detail.

Using IAM in a data lakehouse

The first component for the data security layer is IAM, which ensures that the right principal gets access to the right component with the correct authorization level. For example, the principal could be a range of identities, including a person, a device, or an application, that can request an action or operation on a data lakehouse component. The IAM component determines who gets access to what and how.

IAM employs a **Zero-Trust** architecture. Zero trust means that any organization should have no trust in anything or anyone when accessing resources. With zero trust, a breach is assumed. Every user and device is treated as a threat. Therefore, its access level needs to be verified before being granted. The principles of least-privilege access and identity-based security policies are the cornerstone of a zero-trust architecture.

The following figure shows that an organization should have a holistic IAM implementation strategy with at least five elements:

Figure 7.3 – Elements of a holistic IAM strategy

Let's briefly discuss these six elements.

- **Central Identity Management**: One of the critical principles of a zero-trust architecture is managing access to resources at the identity level. Having a central place to manage identities makes IAM implementation straightforward.

- **Secure Access**: In a zero-trust architecture, securing at the identity level is critical. An IAM should make sure that it confirms those who are logging in. Secure access should also consider the context of the login attempt, that is, parameters such as location, time, and devices.

- **Policy-Based Control**: A zero-trust architecture follows the **Principle of Least Privilege** (**POLP**). POLP signifies that the users should only be given enough authorization to perform their required tasks – no more or no less. These policies should also be managed centrally. Managing the policies centrally will ensure that the resources are secure no matter where they are accessed.

- **Zero-Trust Policy**: A zero-trust policy sees an organization with an IAM solution constantly monitor and secure its users' identities and access points. The zero-trust policies ensure that each identity is continuously identified and has its access managed.

- **Secured Privileged Account**: Secured privileged accounts imply that not all identities are created equal. The policy should provide the identities with special tools or access to sensitive information in the appropriate tier of security and support.

Now that we have covered the elements of the IAM implementation strategy, let's discuss how IAM works. The following diagram depicts the working and tasks of IAM:

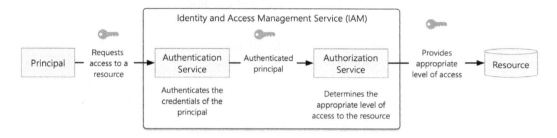

Figure 7.4 – The working of the IAM component

IAM performs a two-step process, authentication and authorization, which is as follows:

1. In the first step, the principal who needs access to a resource sends a request to the **authentication** service of the IAM. Next, the authentication service checks the principal's credentials and recognizes the principal's identity by comparing the credentials with its database. If the credentials are valid, then the principal is authenticated.

2. Once the principal is authenticated, the request goes to the **authorization** service. The authorization service checks the policies of permissions associated with the principal. It determines what level of access needs to be provided to the principal for the resource.

Tools such as password-management tools, provisioning software, security-policy enforcement applications, reporting and monitoring apps, and identity repositories are required to implement a holistic IAM policy. Typical capabilities of an IAM component include the following:

- **Single Sign-On (SSO)**: SSO means accessing all the applications and resources with one sign-in.

- **Multi-Factor Authentication (MFA)**: MFA authenticates using more than one verification method. It adds a second layer of security to user sign-ins.

- **Role-Based Access Control (RBAC)**: RBAC provides fine-grained access management of resources based on specific roles. RBAC assigns roles such as owner, contributor, reader, administrator, and so on, and allows you to granularly control users' level of access.

- **Monitoring and alerts**: This IAM functionality enables security monitoring alerts, and machine learning-based reports identifying inconsistent access patterns.

- **Device registration**: Device registration provides conditional access to devices. When a device is registered, IAM offers the device an identity to authenticate the device.

- **Identity protection**: Identity protection facilitates monitoring potential risks and vulnerabilities that affect the organization's identities.

- **Privileged identity management**: IAM should perform privileged identity management that enables the management, control, and monitoring of privileged identities and access to resources.

Now that we have covered the first component of the data security layer, let's discuss the second component, the **data encryption service**.

Methods of data encryption in a data lakehouse

The second data security component is the data encryption service. Encryption is the most common form of protecting data. When data is encrypted, it cannot be deciphered even if someone gains unauthorized access to it. It becomes the second line of defense. However, hackers have their methods as well. They are getting more and more sophisticated in breaching data. The standard method of attacking encryption is through **brute force**. Brute force tries multiple keys to gain access to data until the right one is found. The encryption algorithms that encrypt the data prevent this by employing sophisticated algorithms and smartly managing its keys.

The following figure depicts the data encryption process:

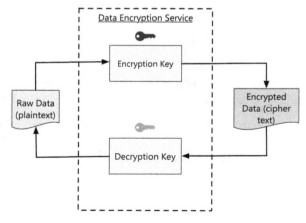

Figure 7.5 – The high-level process of data encryption

Data encryption is the process of translating data from typical data in **human-readable format (plaintext)** into a format that is **unreadable by humans (ciphertext)**. An encryption algorithm performs this translation. Once the data is encrypted, it needs to be decrypted to be human-readable again. A decryption key decodes the ciphertext back into plaintext.

There are two types of encryption algorithms – **symmetric** and **asymmetric**:

- **Symmetric encryption**: In symmetric encryption, both the encryption and decryption keys are the same. Therefore, you must use the same key to enable secure communication. Symmetric algorithms are fast and can be easily implemented, and hence they are used for bulk data encryption. However, since both the encryption and decryption keys are the same, they can be read by anyone who has the key. The key will also need to be shared for it to be used to decrypt data.

- **Asymmetric encryption**: Asymmetric algorithms have a more complex implementation. The working of an asymmetric algorithm differs from that of a symmetric algorithm. In asymmetric algorithm encryption, two separate keys that are mathematically linked are used. One key, a public key, is used to encrypt the data and can be distributed. The other key is a private key used to decrypt the data. Using a private key means the need to exchange secret keys is eliminated, making it more secure. However, it is slower than the symmetric algorithm and requires greater computational power.

You can use many sophisticated algorithms to encrypt data. A few algorithms that are commonly used are as follows:

- **The Advanced Encryption Standard (AES)**: AES is the trusted standard algorithm used by the United States government and other organizations. AES can use different bits of keys for encryption. A 128-bit key is considered very sophisticated, and 256-bit keys are used for a demanding encryption process. Therefore, many cloud computing vendors use AES 256-bit encryption to encrypt data. In addition, AES is broadly considered immune to all attacks except for brute force.

- **Rivest-Shamir-Adleman (RSA)**: RSA is another asymmetric encryption algorithm. It uses a factorization method that uses factors of the product of two large prime numbers. This technique means hackers find decoding the data more challenging. To decrypt the message, the hacker or the user needs to be aware of these prime numbers. However, the challenge with RSA is the speed of encryption. It slows down as the volume of data grows.

- **Blowfish**: The **Data Encryption Standard (DES)** algorithm was a symmetric-key block cipher created in the early 1970s. The working of the algorithm includes taking plaintext in 64-bit blocks and converting it into ciphertext using 48-bit keys. However, since it's a symmetric-key algorithm, it employs the same key in encrypting and decrypting the data. Over time, DES's popularity declined as it was found that hackers could repeatedly breach it. As a result, many new sophisticated algorithms were designed to replace DES, and Blowfish is one of them. Blowfish is a symmetric algorithm as well. This algorithm breaks the messages into 64-bit blocks. Once broken, each block is encrypted individually. Blowfish has established a reputation for speed and flexibility and is unbreakable. It is commonly found on e-commerce platforms, for securing payments and password management tools.

- **Twofish**: Twofish is Blowfish's successor and is license-free, symmetric encryption. Unlike Blowfish, it deciphers 128-bit data blocks instead of 64-bit blocks. On top of that, Twofish encrypts data in 16 rounds irrespective of the critical size. As a result, Twofish is perfect for both software and hardware environments and is considered one of the fastest of its type.

In the context of the data lakehouse, these encryption algorithms are used to protect the data in the **data lake layer and data serving layer, that is, data at rest**. In addition, you can protect data in motion by applying **Transport Layer Security (TLS)**. TLS provides three layers of security – encryption, data integrity, and authentication. The **Hypertext Transfer Protocol Secure (HTTPS)** protocol uses TLS to secure communication over various networks, including the internet.

Let's now move on to the next component used to mask data.

Methods of data masking in a data lakehouse

A data lakehouse can contain a lot of sensitive data that needs protection from unauthorized access. This could include **Personally Identifiable Information (PII)** such as social security numbers, email, or phone numbers, or sensitive information such as credit card or bank account numbers. Not everyone needs to access this sensitive data. A data masking service adds a layer of protection to ensure that sensitive data is only accessed by the most privileged users with the need to access it. Data masking is a way to create an artificial but practical version of data. It protects sensitive data without sacrificing the functionality that it offers. There are several reasons why data masking is vital for an organization:

- Data masking mitigates external and internal threats. For example, data exfiltration, insider threats or account compromise, and insecure interfaces with third-party systems are some threats mitigated by data masking.

- Data masking makes data useless to the attacker, as it veils its actual content without compromising the inherent functional properties.

- Data masking enables secured data sharing between the production version of data and the data required to test or develop software.

Data masking is different from encryption. Encryption is done at the data store level, whereas data masking is only applied to the specific data elements that are deemed sensitive. Let's now discuss different types of data masking:

- **Static Data Masking**: The first type of data masking is **Static Data Masking** (**SDM**). The following figure depicts the process of SDM:

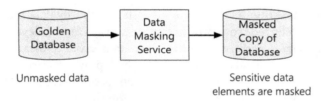

Figure 7.6 – The process of SDM

The golden database has unmasked data. The data masking service creates a copy of the database by masking the sensitive information. You can then use this masked copy of the database for other purposes. Typically, the golden database is the production copy. The masked version of the database is used for development and testing.

- **Dynamic Data Masking**: Another type of data masking is **Dynamic Data Masking** (**DDM**). The following figure depicts the process of DDM:

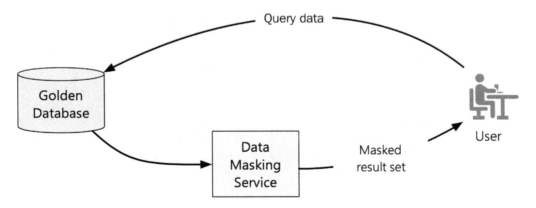

Figure 7.7 – The process of DDM

DDM happens at runtime. First, the data is streamed from the golden database. While the data is streamed, data masking services mask the sensitive data on the fly. DDM employs RBAC, which determines whether the user accessing the data has the privilege to see the sensitive data. If the user doesn't have the privilege to see the data, the data masking service masks the data before providing access to the user. DDM applies to read-only scenarios to prevent writing the masked data back to the production system.

- **Deterministic data masking**: Deterministic data masking maps two sets of data. Then, the original dataset is replaced by another dataset with the same data type. For example, *Jack Reacher* might always be replaced with *Tom Cruise* in all the columns of a database.

- **On-the-fly data masking**: As the name suggests, on-the-fly data masking masks data while it is transferred from production systems to test or development systems. The masking activity is performed before the data is saved to disk. This type of data masking is used by organizations that frequently deploy software. Creating a backup copy of the source database for every deployment is not feasible. Instead, they need to continuously stream data from production to other environments such as development and testing.

Now that we have discussed the different types of data masking, let's look into different techniques that you can use to mask data. The following figure depicts commonly used data masking techniques:

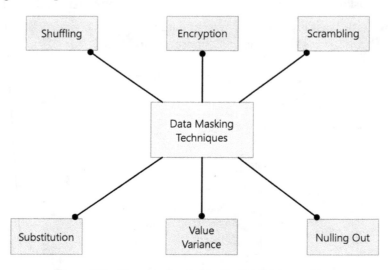

Figure 7.8 – Commonly used methods of data masking

Let's discuss these techniques briefly:

- **Encryption**: We covered encryption in detail in the last section. You can also use any of those encryption methods for data masking.

- **Scrambling**: Scrambling is a basic masking technique that jumbles the characters and numbers into a random order, thus hiding the original content. For example, an ID number of 1234 in a production database could be replaced by 4321 in a test database.

- **Nulling Out**: The nulling out data masking technique replaces the sensitive data with a null value so that unauthorized users don't see the actual data. The data appears to be *null* or missing.

- **Value Variance**: Original data values are replaced by a function that replaces the original data with the output value of the function. For example, suppose a customer purchases several products. In that case, the masking method can replace the purchase price with a range between the highest and lowest price paid.

- **Substitution**: In the substitution data masking technique, the sensitive data is substituted with another value. The substitution technique is one of the most effective data masking methods, which preserves the original look, such asthe look and feel of the data.

- **Shuffling**: The data shuffling technique involves moving data within rows in the same column. This technique is like substitution. However, the data values are switched within the same dataset in this case. The data is rearranged in each column using a random sequence.

Now that we have covered data masking, let's move on to the last component of the data security layer, that is, the network security service.

Methods of implementing network security in a data lakehouse

The network is the lifeline of the data lakehouse. The data flows in and out of the data lakehouse through the network. The network acts as a conduit to other systems as well. Therefore, it is paramount to ensure that the network is well protected. All other data security components work in tandem with network security services. Network security aims to protect the usability and integrity of your network. It effectively manages access to the network and mitigates various threats and stops them from entering or spreading on your network.

In the previous section, we covered the network security layer at a high level. So, let's further drill down to the network security service and discuss what it entails. The following figure dives deeper into the subcomponents of network security services:

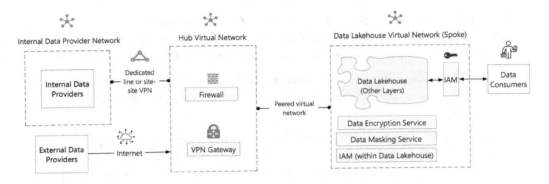

Figure 7.9 – The subcomponents of network security services

Let's break down this figure based on the subcomponents:

- **Virtual Network**: The first subcomponent of the network security service is the **Virtual Network (VNET)**. A virtual network connects all devices, servers, virtual machines, and data centers through software and wireless technology. A typical implementation of VNETs includes a **hub-spoke** network topology. The virtual hub network is the central point of connectivity to the external network. It is a place to host services that are consumed by different workloads that are hosted in the virtual spoke networks. The spoke virtual networks isolate workloads in their virtual networks and are managed separately from other spokes. For example, the components of the data lakehouse are secured within its **spoke** VNET.

- **Firewall**: A hub VNET has specialized network security subcomponents that control the access to the spoke VNETs, including the data lakehouse VNET. That brings us to the second subcomponent of the network security layer, the **firewall**. A firewall is a network security component that watches and filters incoming and outgoing network traffic. Its primary purpose is to allow non-threatening traffic and keep dangerous traffic out. It screens this traffic based on an organization's previously established security policies. It acts as a barrier between a private internal network and the public internet. It also prevents malicious software from accessing a computer or network via the internet. Firewalls can also be configured to allow only specific devices, applications, or ports to allow communication.

- **Virtual Private Network (VPN) gateway**: The network traffic flows between the external and the data lakehouse networks. The data packets that flow through these networks need to be encrypted. That brings us to the third subcomponent of the network security layer, the **VPN gateway**. A VPN gateway is used to send encrypted traffic between the data lakehouse's virtual network and other networks that are external to the data lakehouse networks. These networks can be an organization's own data center networks or locations over the public internet.

We have covered all the components of the data security layer. Let's now conclude by summarizing the key aspects of this chapter.

Summary

This chapter covered the components of the data security layer, one of the essential layers of a data lakehouse. Data security is paramount in any system. Its importance is accentuated when it comes to protecting data **access**, **usage**, and **storage**. This chapter covered how to secure data and ensure that the right access is provided at the right layer to the right stakeholder. The chapter began by giving an overview of the four components of the data security layer. Then, we discussed how these four layers interact with each other. The following sections of the chapter delved deeper into each component. The first component discussed was **IAM**. IAM ensures that the right user gets access to the right component with the correct authorization level. We also discussed the principles of **zero-trust** architecture. The following section discussed the ways data can be encrypted in a data lakehouse using a data encryption service. When the data is encrypted, it cannot be deciphered, even if someone gains unauthorized access to data. Then, we discussed the various encryption methods that can be employed to secure data, and we also covered the ways data can be masked in a data lakehouse using a data masking service. Data masking allows us to hide sensitive information and ensures that access to such information is provided prudently. We discussed various methods used in data masking in this section.

The final section of the chapter focused on network security services. Network security binds the data flow within and outside of the data lakehouse. This section discussed three key subcomponents of network security services that protect data and its access.

We have covered all seven layers of the data lakehouse with this chapter. The next chapter will focus on the practical implementation of a data lakehouse using a cloud computing platform.

Further reading

For more information regarding the topics that were covered in this chapter, take a look at the following resources:

- *Identity and Access Management*: `https://digitalguardian.com/blog/what-identity-and-access-management-iam`

- *Identity and Access Management 101*: `https://www.okta.com/identity-101/identity-and-access-management/`

- *Identity and Access Management*: `https://docs.microsoft.com/en-us/azure/security/fundamentals/identity-management-overview`

- *Identity and Access Management*: `https://www.onelogin.com/learn`

- *Data Encryption*: `https://digitalguardian.com/blog/what-data-encryption`

- *Data Encryption*: `https://www.forcepoint.com/cyber-edu/data-encryption`

- *Fundamentals of Data Encryption*: `https://docs.microsoft.com/en-us/azure/security/fundamentals/encryption-atrest`

- *What is Encryption*: `https://us.norton.com/internetsecurity-privacy-what-is-encryption.html`

- *Common Storage Encryption*: `https://docs.microsoft.com/en-us/azure/storage/common/storage-service-encryption?toc=/azure/storage/blobs/toc.json`

- *Symmetric Key Encryption*: `https://www.cryptomathic.com/news-events/blog/symmetric-key-encryption-why-where-and-how-its-used-in-banking`

- *Encryption Methods*: `https://www.simplilearn.com/data-encryption-methods-article`

- *Encryption Overview*: `https://docs.microsoft.com/en-us/azure/security/fundamentals/encryption-overview`

- *Transport Layer Security*: `https://en.wikipedia.org/wiki/Transport_Layer_Security`

- *Securing with HTTPS*: `https://developers.google.com/search/docs/advanced/security/https`

- *Data Masking*: `https://www.imperva.com/learn/data-security/data-masking/`

- *Data Masking*: https://www.bmc.com/blogs/data-masking/

- *Data Masking*: https://www.datprof.com/solutions/deterministic-data-masking/

- *Data Masking*: https://www.delphix.com/glossary/data-masking

- *Virtual Networks*: https://docs.microsoft.com/en-us/azure/virtual-network/virtual-networks-overview

- *Firewall*: https://us.norton.com/internetsecurity-emerging-threats-what-is-firewall

- *Understanding Firewalls*: https://us-cert.cisa.gov/ncas/tips/ST04-004

- *Virtual Networks*: https://www.bmc.com/blogs/virtual-network/#

- *Network Hub-Spoke*: https://docs.microsoft.com/en-us/azure/architecture/reference-architectures/hybrid-networking/hub-spoke?tabs=cli

- *Firewalls*: https://www.checkpoint.com/cyber-hub/network-security/what-is-firewall/

- *VPN Gateway*: https://www.techopedia.com/definition/30755/vpn-gateway

PART 3: Implementing and Governing a Data Lakehouse

This section focuses on the cloud services used to implement and govern a data lakehouse. It will explain the services in Microsoft Azure that you can use with your data lakehouse architecture, the need for a macro architecture pattern for your data lakehouse, and the organizational drivers that dictate the requirements for such a pattern. Then, the section will cover two types of macro architecture patterns, hub-spoke and data mesh, and discuss the concepts of these macro patterns and how the idea of the data lakehouse interlaces with these patterns.

This section comprises the following chapters:

- *Chapter 8, Implementing a Data Lakehouse on Microsoft Azure*
- *Chapter 9, Scaling the Data Lakehouse Architecture*

8
Implementing a Data Lakehouse on Microsoft Azure

We have come a long way on our journey in exploring modern data analytics architecture through the concept of the data lakehouse. All seven layers of the data lakehouse are covered in detail in the preceding chapters. Although you can employ the same architecture in any cloud service or even on-premises, I will implement a data lakehouse on the **Microsoft Azure platform**.

This chapter will start by refreshing the concepts covered in *Chapter 1, Introducing the Evolution of Data Analytics Patterns*, and *Chapter 2, The Data Lakehouse Architecture Overview*, and establishing the advantages of using cloud computing. The following three sections of the chapter will focus on the cloud services used to bring to fruition the data lakehouse architecture. Finally, the chapter will explain the services in Microsoft Azure that you can use to realize the data lakehouse architecture. We will discuss the key features of each of these services, the rationale for selecting one service over another, and the potential alternatives for given specific scenarios.

All cloud computing platforms are continually evolving and innovating. As a result, the appropriate service to achieve a particular functionality is also evolving. We will consider services in Azure that are current at the time of writing this chapter, that is, the fourth quarter of 2021.

We will be asking the following questions in the chapter:

- Why is cloud computing apt for implementing a data lakehouse?
- What are the services used to implement a data lakehouse on Microsoft Azure?

Let's get started by discussing the first of those questions: *why is cloud computing apt for implementing a data lakehouse?*

Why is cloud computing apt for implementing a data lakehouse?

Why cloud computing is apt for implementing a data lakehouse has been discussed in previous chapters. This section will recap and consolidate the top three reasons for adopting **cloud computing** for a data lakehouse.

The rapid advancements in cloud computing facilitate data analytics

Recall that in *Chapter 1, Introducing the Evolution of Data Analytics Patterns*, we discussed the *five factors* that have caused the perfect *data storm*. The following figure recaps these five factors:

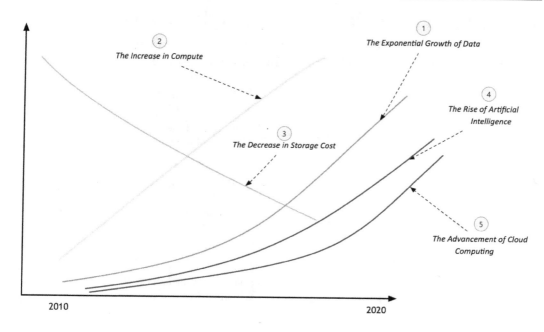

Figure 8.1 – Ingredients of the perfect data storm

One of the five factors was **The Advancement of Cloud Computing**. As discussed extensively in *Chapter 1, Introducing the Evolution of Data Analytics Patterns*, the cloud computing landscape has constantly risen since 2010. Worldwide spending on the public cloud started at around $77 billion in 2010 and reached around $441 billion in 2020. Cloud computing eliminates the need to host large servers for computing and storage on an organization's data center. Depending on the service in the cloud, organizations can also reduce their dependencies on software and hardware maintenance.

Cloud computing also has been a boon for data. Here, I will reiterate the discussion from *Chapter 1, Introducing the Evolution of Data Analytics Patterns*. With the rise of cloud computing, you can now store data at a fraction of the previous cost. In addition, the more or less limitless compute power that the cloud provides translates into the ability to transform data rapidly. Finally, cloud computing also provides innovative data platforms that organizations can utilize at the click of a button.

Architectural flexibility is native to the cloud

Recall that in *Chapter 2, The Data Lakehouse Architecture Overview*, we discussed **architecture principles** for the data lakehouse. The following figure recaps these principles:

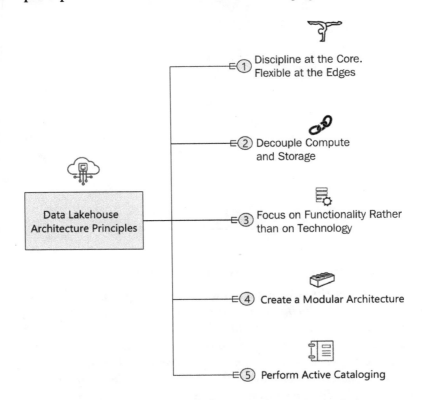

Figure 8.2 – The data lakehouse architecture principles

The two fundamental principles of decoupling compute and storage and creating a modular architecture are native to cloud computing platforms. As you may recall from the discussions in *Chapter 2, The Data Lakehouse Architecture Overview*, a data lakehouse stores data in structured and unstructured formats. The data needs to be processed using different types of compute engines. Decoupling compute and storage provides the flexibility of spinning up compute services on-demand and scaling it as required.

The other principle of **creating a modular architecture** is also native to the cloud. As discussed in *Chapter 2, The Data Lakehouse Architecture Overview*, a modular architecture refers to designing any system composed of separate components that can connect. A modular architecture ensures that the data lakehouse architecture is created flexibly. You can add new functionality seamlessly without breaking the existing functionality.

Cloud computing enables tailored cost control

The third factor that calls for cloud computing for the data lakehouse is *the cloud platforms' tailored cost control*. As a cloud computing platform provides decoupling of compute and storage, it also offers the flexibility of utilizing the compute on-demand. Typically, the cost of computing is more expensive than the cost of storage. In all cloud computing platforms, compute engines can be paused when not in use. This feature enables tailored cost control, depending on the compute requirements.

In addition, many data analytics-related services in the cloud computing world are **Platform as a Service (PaaS)**. PaaS means you do not need to manage the underlying hardware. Instead, the management of the underlying hardware is the responsibility of the cloud platform provider. Moreover, PaaS services have built-in features such as **High Availability (HA)** and on-demand scalability essential for data analytics services.

Now that we have covered the top three reasons for adopting **cloud computing** for the data lakehouse, let's recap its **logical architecture**. The following figure refreshes the logical architecture of the data lakehouse:

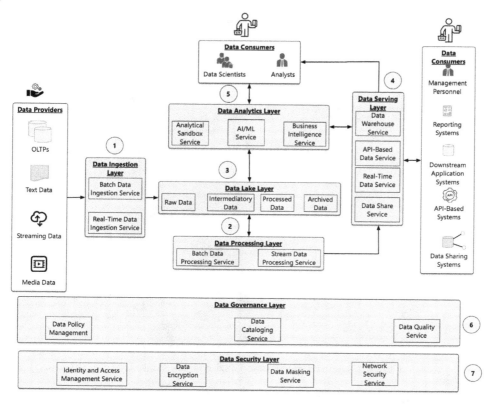

Figure 8.3 – The data lakehouse logical architecture

In the subsequent sections, we will explore the services that you can use to bring to fruition each layer of the data lakehouse architecture for Microsoft Azure.

Implementing a data lakehouse on Microsoft Azure

The following figure maps the key cloud services available in Microsoft Azure for each of the seven layers of a data lakehouse:

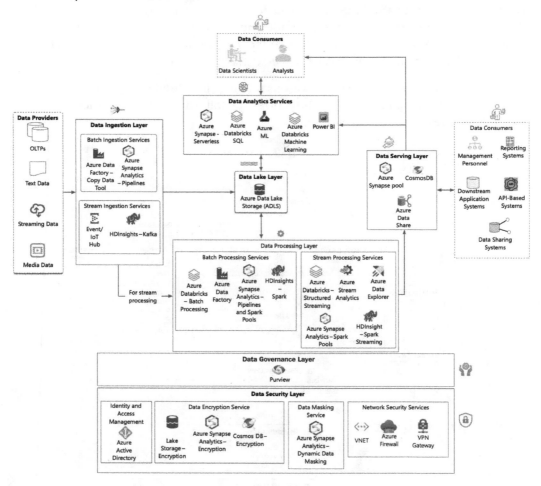

Figure 8.4 – Azure services that realize data lakehouse layers

Each of these services has a plethora of features. Deep-diving into each of these services is beyond the scope of this book. However, we will explore each of these services in brief. It will also be prudent to note the following for Azure data services:

One service is designed to fulfill multiple functionalities. Here, we will discuss specific features of the most convenient services frequently used to realize a particular component of the data lakehouse architecture.

The data ingestion layer on Microsoft Azure

The first layer is the data ingestion layer. Recall that in *Chapter 3, Ingesting and Processing Data in a Data Lakehouse*, we covered the architectural considerations of the data ingestion layer. This layer is the integration point for the external data provided to the data lakehouse. This section will explore key Microsoft Azure services that you can use to realize the data ingestion layer.

The following figure depicts the key Microsoft Azure services that you can use for data ingestion:

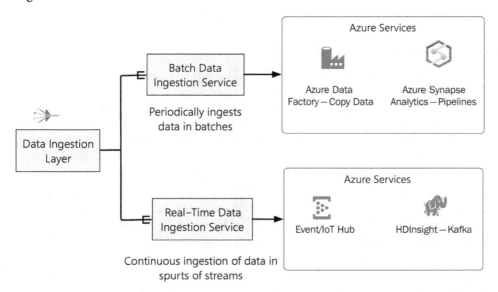

Figure 8.5 – The data ingestion services on Azure

The Azure services, **Azure Data Factory – Copy Data**, **Azure Synapse Analytics – Pipelines**, **Event/IoT Hub**, and **HDInsight – Kafka**, are the major services that you can use to realize the data ingestion layer. All these services are PaaS on Azure. The choice of service depends on the specific use case, the non-functional requirements, and the existing skill sets within the organization.

Batch data ingestion services

Let's investigate the different types of ingestion services in a little more detail:

- **Azure Data Factory (ADF)**: ADF is a fully managed, serverless data integration service. It enables the integration of data sources with more than 90 built-in maintenance-free connectors. ADF facilitates the easy construction of ETL and ELT data flow in a code-free and intuitive environment. It also enables you to write your own code. In addition, ADF has a functionality called **Copy Data tool** that can ingest batch data from many data sources with a few clicks.

- **Azure Synapse Analytics pipelines**: Azure Synapse Analytics is an Azure service that strives to create a **unified analytics platform** to provide a seamless customer experience. It facilitates end-to-end analytics, including data integration, processing, storage, serving, and analytics. Synapse pipelines are the part of Synapse Analytics that perform the data integration part. They use ADF as their engine. The data integration workflow can be created using Synapse Studio, which facilitates the development of these pipelines without leaving the Synapse user experience.

Let's now investigate the options for stream data ingestion.

Stream data ingestion services

There are two key Azure services that can be used for stream data ingestion. Let's drill into them in detail:

- **Event Hubs/IoT Hub**: For stream data ingestion, Azure Event Hubs is frequently used. It is a fully managed, real-time data ingestion service that can scale seamlessly. Based on the service tier, it can stream millions of events per second from any source. It also has in-built high availability and features such as geo-disaster recovery and geo-replication. Azure Event Hubs also allows existing Apache Kafka clients and applications to talk to Event Hubs without code changes. Another messaging service offered by Azure is Azure **Internet of Things (IoT)** Hub. Azure IoT Hub enables highly secure and reliable communication between IoT applications and devices. It allows a cloud-hosted service to connect any device virtually. Azure IoT Hub facilitates communication from the cloud to the edge with per-device authentication, built-in device management, and scaled provisioning.

- **HDInsight – Kafka:** The other option available for message queuing is to explore Apache Kafka on **HDInsight (HDI)**. Apache Kafka is an open source, distributed streaming platform that builds real-time streaming data pipelines and applications. Kafka also provides message broker functionality such as a message queue. In addition, you can publish and subscribe to named data streams. HDInsight delivers a platform to run popular open source frameworks, including Apache Hadoop, Spark, Hive, and Kafka, to name a few. It is a customizable, enterprise-grade service for open source analytics. With HDInsight, you can effortlessly process massive amounts of data and get all the benefits of the broad open source project ecosystem in a scalable manner.

Now that we have covered the data ingestion services, let's focus on the data processing services.

The data processing layer on Microsoft Azure

The second layer is the **data processing layer**. Recall that in *Chapter 3, Ingesting and Processing Data in a Data Lakehouse*, we covered the architectural considerations of the data processing layer. The data needs to be transformed or processed to be consumed for insights. Data processing services perform the job of converting data ingested into a form that can serve the stakeholders. This section will explore key Microsoft Azure services that an organization can use to realize the data processing layer:

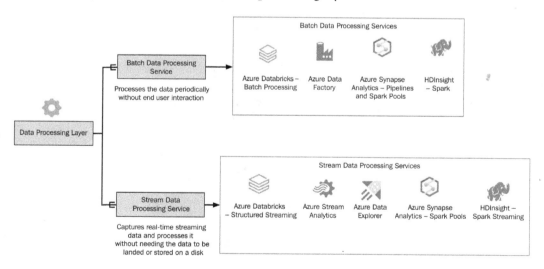

Figure 8.6 – The data processing services on Azure

The preceding figure depicts the different types of Azure data services that you can use for data processing. In addition, you can use some of the services, such as Azure Databricks, for both batch and stream processing. Let's investigate each of these services in brief.

Batch data processing services

Now, let's discuss the key Azure services that are used for batch data processing:

- **Azure Databricks**: Databricks is a company founded by the developers of Spark. Databricks offers a commercial version of open source Spark that is further optimized for data engineering and data science. Azure Databricks is the jointly developed **data and AI service** from Databricks and Microsoft. It has a powerful data processing engine with optimized **Spark** and an open format storage layer called **Delta Lake**. Azure Databricks also leverages **Azure Data Lake Storage (ADLS)** to process streaming and batch data at scale with almost zero maintenance. Azure Databricks also provides a platform for end-to-end life cycle management of data engineering and data science workloads using collaborative workspaces and notebooks. Finally, it provides best-in-class security features, including compliance, identity and access integration, and encryption.

- **Azure Data Factory– data flow**: We discussed the capability of ADF to ingest data into Azure. It also can enable data transformations. ADF offers **data flows**. Azure Data Factory's data flow module enables the creation of data transformations through a drag and drop interface. It allows data engineers to develop data transformation logic without writing code. Instead, the visually designed codes are executed as Azure Data Factory pipelines using scaled-out Apache Spark clusters. Data flow activities can also be operationalized using existing Azure Data Factory scheduling, control, flow, and monitoring capabilities.

- **Azure Synapse Analytics – pipelines and Spark pools**: We briefly discussed the ability of Azure Synapse to ingest data using Synapse pipelines. Since Synapse pipelines use ADF as their engine, ADF's data flows are also available within Synapse pipelines. Azure Synapse Analytics also provides Spark pools that you can use for data transformation. Synapse Spark pools are serverless and are created when you connect to a Spark pool, create a session, and run a job. Organizations can use these Spark instances for data transformation using Spark.

- **HDInsight – Spark:** The other option for data processing is to utilize Spark clusters offered by HDI. As discussed earlier, HDInsight provides a platform to run popular open source frameworks, including Apache Hadoop, Spark, Hive, and Kafka, to name a few. Apache Spark is a parallel processing framework that supports in-memory processing. Spark is predominantly used to boost the performance of big-data analytic applications. Apache Spark in Azure HDInsight leverages a cloud computing infrastructure and is the Microsoft implementation of open source Apache Spark. Thus, HDInsight makes it easier to create and configure a Spark cluster in Azure. In addition, spark clusters in HDInsight are compatible with ADLS.

Let's now look into the services available on the Azure platform to enable stream data processing.

Stream data processing services

There are three key services in Azure that are optimized for stream data processing. Let's discuss them in a little more detail:

- **Azure Databricks:** Databricks also supports Spark's **Structured Streaming**. Structured Streaming is a scalable and fault-tolerant stream processing engine built on the Spark SQL engine.

- **Azure Stream Analytics:** If the requirement is to use a SQL-based stream processing engine, then Azure Stream Analytics is an excellent service to use. Azure Stream Analytics is an easy-to-use, real-time analytics service designed for mission-critical workloads using SQL. Azure Stream Analytics can also extend custom code and built-in machine learning capabilities for more advanced scenarios. This capability gives developers more control for programming streaming data. Being a PaaS, it provides the required scalability with a built-in elastic capacity that enables the analysis of millions of events with low latencies. In addition, Azure Stream Analytics excels in hybrid architecture scenarios where there is a need to run the same queries in the cloud and on the edge.

- **Azure Data Explorer (ADX)**: ADX is another stream processing service offered by Azure. It enables real-time analysis on large volumes of data streaming from applications, websites, and IoT devices, to name a few. ADX uses **Kusto Query Language (KQL)**, which enables you to explore data iteratively and on the fly. ADX supports fast low-latency ingestion with linear scaling that supports up to 200 MB of data per second per node. ADX's KQL enables you to query large amounts of structured, semi-structured (JSON-like nested types), and unstructured (free-text) data. It allows searching for specific text terms, locating events, and performing calculations on structured data. ADX also includes native support for the creation, manipulation, and analysis of multiple time series. The major use cases for ADX include normalizing and aggregating data from IoT devices and analyzing large volumes of log data to spot trends, patterns, or anomalies in near real time.

Now, let's move to the next layer and discuss how a data lake can be enabled on Azure.

The data lake layer on Microsoft Azure

The third layer is the **data lake layer**. Recall that in *Chapter 4, Storing and Serving Data in a Data Lakehouse*, we discussed the need for the data lake layer. Once the data ingestion layer ingests the data, it needs to be landed into storage. Next, various transformations need to be performed to transform the data for consumption. Finally, the data is anchored in the data lake. This section will explore the key Microsoft Azure service that you can use to realize the data lake layer.

The following figure illustrates the different types of data stores in the data lake layer. All the data stores can be realized using **Azure Data Lake Storage (ADLS)** in Azure:

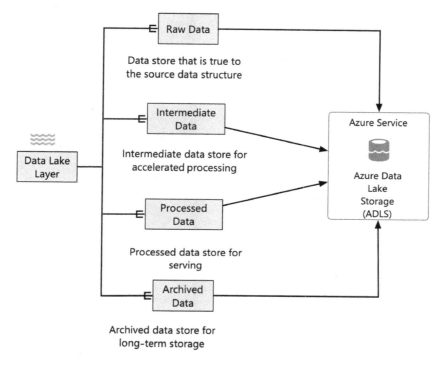

Figure 8.7 – The data processing services on Azure

ADLS is a massively scalable and secure data lake for high-performance analytics workloads. It is designed for big data workloads and is compatible with the **Hadoop Distributed File System (HDFS)** file structure. Recall that in *Chapter 4, Storing and Serving Data in a Data Lakehouse,* we discussed *hierarchical file structures.* A hierarchical file structure creates a folder that behaves more like a traditional OS filesystem regarding moving and renaming. ADLS supports storing data in a hierarchical file structure. ADLS also supports efficient cost optimization using tiered storage and policy management. ADLS also can take advantage of automated life cycle management policies for optimizing storage costs. For example, it can be automatically moved from *hot* to *cold* to *archival* storage. In addition, ADLS provides the mechanism to authenticate data using **Azure Active Directory (Azure AD)** and **Role-Based Access Control (RBAC)**. It also helps to protect data with security features such as encryption at rest and advanced threat protection. Recall that in *Chapter 2, The Data Lakehouse Architecture Overview,* we discussed the five *architectural principles* associated with the data lakehouse. One of the principles was decoupling compute and storage. ADLS can also optimize costs by scaling storage and compute power independently.

Let's now move on to the next layer and discuss the Azure services that can implement the data serving layer.

The data serving layer on Microsoft Azure

The fourth layer is the **data serving layer**. Recall that in *Chapter 4, Storing and Serving Data in a Data Lakehouse*, we discussed the need for the data serving layer. Once the data is processed in the data lake, it needs to be served to the downstream applications or stakeholders:

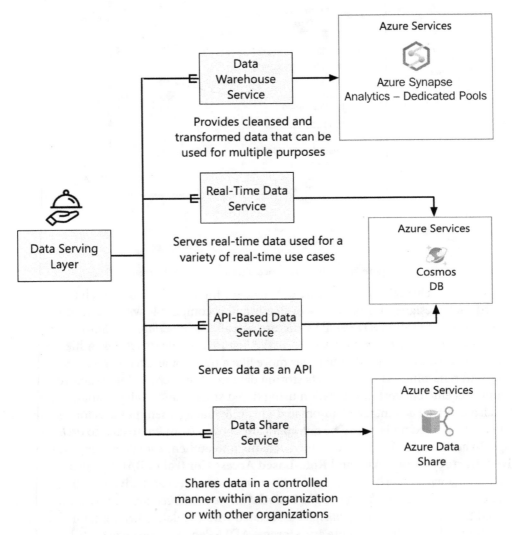

Figure 8.8 – The data serving services on Azure

The preceding figure depicts the key Microsoft Azure services that fulfill various components of the data serving layer. Let's discuss these services in detail.

Data warehouse service

In **Azure Synapse Analytics – Dedicated Pools**, Microsoft used to offer a **SQL Data Warehouse (SQL DW)** product. That product has now evolved as a Synapse Analytics feature called **dedicated SQL pool**.

Recall that in *Chapter 4, Storing and Serving Data in a Data Lakehouse*, we discussed the concept of a **Symmetric Multi-Processor (SMP)** and **Massively Parallel Processing (MPP)** architecture. An MPP-based architecture employs a *share-nothing* architecture by slicing the data into multiple chunks and processes each chunk independently. Synapse's dedicated pool does just that. MPP leverages a scale-out architecture to distribute computational data processing across multiple nodes. The unit of scale is an abstraction of compute power that is known as a **data warehouse unit**. It employs the principle of separating compute from storage that enables you to scale compute independently of the data storage.

In the MPP-based architecture of Azure Synapse, the data is stored in Azure Storage. The performance is optimized by sharding the data across multiple distributions based on algorithms such as **round-robin distribution**, **hash distribution**, or **replication**. The **compute nodes** provide the computational power, and the data distributions map to the compute nodes for processing. Azure Synapse achieves horizontal scaling as you increase the number of compute nodes. A control node interacts with all applications and connections. The distributed query engine runs on the control node to optimize and coordinate parallel queries. The Synapse Analytics dedicated SQL pool is used as the **data warehouse** or **data mart** and serves reporting and advanced analytics use cases.

Let's now discuss the ways to realize a real-time data service.

Real-time data service/API-based data service

Azure Cosmos DB enables real-time data serving and exposes data as an API. Let's discuss this service in detail.

Azure Cosmos DB is a fully managed, globally distributed NoSQL database service that provides low latency, elastic scalability of throughput, well-defined semantics for data consistency, and high availability. It enables running near real-time analytics on the operational data within the NoSQL database. It offers multiple database APIs that can be enabled based on the user requirements. The APIs include the Core (SQL) API, the MongoDB API, the Cassandra API, the Gremlin API, and the Table API. Using these APIs, you can model real-world data using documents, key values, graphs, and column-family data models. Moreover, being a globally distributed database system allows reading and writing data from the local replicas. Cosmos DB also transparently replicates the data to all the regions associated with the Cosmos DB account.

Therefore, distributed databases that rely on replication for high availability, low latency, or both must make a fundamental trade-off between the read consistency, availability, latency, and throughput. Azure Cosmos DB offers five well-defined levels, that is, *strong, bounded staleness, session, consistent prefix, and eventual,* in the order of highest consistency to the lowest. Azure Cosmos DB also provides a REST API that enables programmatic access to the underlying data. The predominant use cases that Cosmos DB fulfills are real-time analytics in *IoT-based scenarios* and low-latency downstream applications that require high throughput such as e-commerce platforms.

Let's now discuss the Azure service that enables data sharing.

The Data Share service

As organizations mature, a common theme is the ability to share data internally, that is, selectively and securely within the organization, and externally, that is, with partner ecosystems. Data sharing also provides an avenue to *monetize data.* **Azure Data Share** enables sharing data from multiple sources within the organization or with other organizations in any format and any size. It allows easy control of what data to share, who receives the data, and data use terms.

Data Share provides complete visibility of the data-sharing relationships with a user-friendly interface. It enables efficient tracking of managing the data-sharing relationships. It easily allows integrating the downstream application using the REST API.

Let's now move on to the next layer and discuss which Azure services can be used to realize the data analytics layer.

The data analytics layer on Microsoft Azure

The fifth layer is the **data analytics layer**. Recall that in *Chapter 5, Deriving Insights from a Data Lakehouse,* we covered the analytics layer in detail. Transforming the underlying data into insights is the core of any data analytics platform. The **analytics sandbox services facilitate** ad hoc queries, the **ai/ml services** provide advanced analytics capabilities, and finally, the **Business Intelligence Service** offers reporting and visualization capabilities:

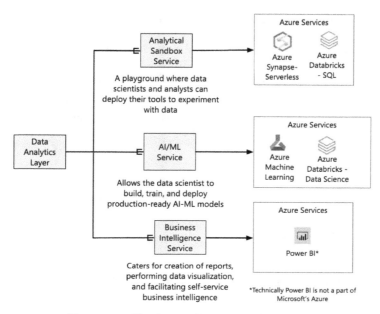

Figure 8.9 – The data analytics services on Azure

The preceding figure depicts the key Microsoft Azure services that fulfill various components of the Data Analytics Layer. Let's discuss them in detail.

Analytical Sandbox Service includes the following:

- **Azure Synapse Analytics – serverless SQL pool**: Azure Synapse Analytics has a **serverless SQL pool** feature that realizes the **analytics sandbox component**. Serverless SQL pool is a query service that queries data in the data lake using Synapse's distributed data processing system. As the name implies, serverless SQL pool is serverless, and there is no underlying infrastructure to maintain. It uses SQL to query the underlying data in the data lake. A default endpoint for this service is provided within every Azure Synapse workspace. The users can start querying data as soon as the workspace is created. The cost model is pay-per-use and implies that there is no charge for resources reserved. The only charge is for the data processed by queries that are run.

- **Azure Databricks – SQL**: Azure Databricks was introduced earlier as a Spark-based **data processing engine**. It also has a feature called **Databricks SQL**. This environment is able to run quick ad hoc SQL queries on the data lake layer. These SQL queries run on fully managed SQL endpoints and are sized according to the query latency and the number of concurrent users. This feature of Azure Databricks fulfills the functionality of being an **analytics sandbox** for rapid data exploration using SQL.

Let's now discuss the Azure services that enable machine learning services, **AI/ML Service**:

- **Azure Databricks – Machine Learning**: Azure Databricks also provides **Databricks Machine Learning**, which fulfills the **machine learning** component. Databricks Machine Learning is an integrated end-to-end machine learning platform that uses a Spark engine for machine learning. It enables data scientists to perform an end-to-end machine learning life cycle, that is, model training, feature development and management, and feature and model serving. The key features of Databricks Machine Learning include the following:

  - **Feature Store** enables the cataloging of attributes (also known as *features*). It makes them available for training and serving, increasing reuse.

  - **MLflow** enables the *tracking* of model components and allows the logging of source properties, parameters, metrics, tags, and artifacts related to training a machine learning model.

  - **AutoML** enables the automatic generation of machine learning models from the underlying data and thus accelerates the path from experimentation to production.

  - **Azure Machine Learning (AML)**: This is another service available in Azure that fulfills the machine learning component. AML empowers data scientists and developers with a wide range of productive experiences to build, train, and deploy machine learning models and foster team collaboration. It provides both code-based and GUI-based interfaces and appeals to *citizen data scientists* and *traditional data scientists*. In addition, Azure Machine Learning facilitates **MLOps**, **continuous deployment**, and **monitoring** of machine learning models at scale using automated and reproducible machine learning workflows. Azure Machine Learning also supports open source frameworks and languages, including MLflow, Kubeflow, **Open Neural Network Exchange** (**ONNX**), PyTorch, TensorFlow, Python, and R. You can easily integrate modules from these languages in your machine learning model creation.

As for **Business Intelligence Service**, **Power BI** is an online **Software as a Service** (**SaaS**) service. It is primarily a data visualization and reporting tool that realizes the **Business Intelligence** (**BI**) service in the data lakehouse. It has a gamut of features, such as rich visualization options, a modeling interface, report creations using a drag-and-drop interface, dashboard creation, and report scheduling, to name a few. It also has rich security features such as encryption and user authentication, to name a few. These features are prevalent in all major enterprise BI tools.

The data governance layer on Microsoft Azure

The sixth layer is the **data governance layer**. Recall that in *Chapter 6, Applying Data Governance in a Data Lakehouse*, we discussed the importance of data cataloging and its components in depth. One of the components was data cataloging. Data cataloging ensures that the data lakehouse doesn't become a data swamp. Furthermore, in *Chapter 6*, we discussed the key elements and process of data cataloging. It forms an essential part of the overall data governance framework:

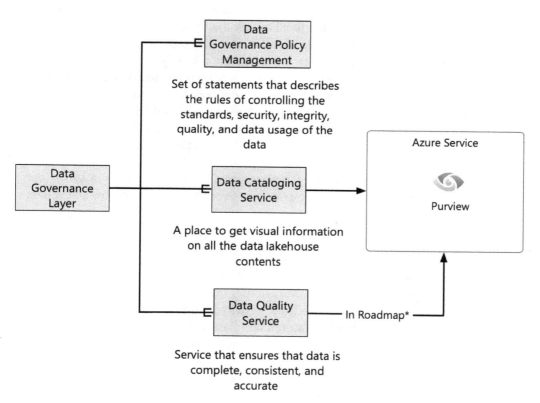

Figure 8.10 – The data cataloging services on Azure

The preceding figure depicts the Azure data services that can realize data cataloging. Let's discuss them in detail.

Data cataloging service and data quality service

Microsoft Azure offers **Azure Purview** as its unified data governance service. At the time of writing this chapter, it provides rich data cataloging features. Purview offers the data catalog and sharing aspect of the data governance framework. The first feature that Purview provides is the **automatic scanning and classification of metadata** from multiple clouds and on-premises. It has more than 25 out-of-the-box connectors and various file formats. The second feature that Purview provides is a **business glossary**. This enables a curated and consistent understanding of business terms and definitions. You can also import glossary terms from existing data dictionaries. The third feature that Azure Purview provides is the **lineage views** of the data life cycle. This feature allows for data provenance with a visual representation of owners, sources, transformation, and life cycles. Its built-in integrations with sources automatically extract lineage. The fourth feature is **catalog insights**. A catalog insight enables you to see where all the organization's data resides across various data sources. It provides insights into the success and failures of scans and a view of changes made to the glossary over time that helps to assess how much coverage the glossary has over your data map. The catalog insights also provide insights about sensitive data within an organization. Examples of sensitive data can be personally identifiable information and credit card information, to name a couple. Finally, Azure Purview also enables a *search and browse* capability. It provides a search engine that can search for terms and view all the data assets related to that search.

The data security layer on Microsoft Azure

The seventh and final layer is the **data security layer**. Data security is a deep and broad topic. Recall that in *Chapter 7, Applying Data Security in a Data Lakehouse*, we discussed the components of data security in detail. Data security is applied across the different layers of the data lakehouse when data is stored and accessed. The following figure depicts the Azure services that can realize specific components of data security:

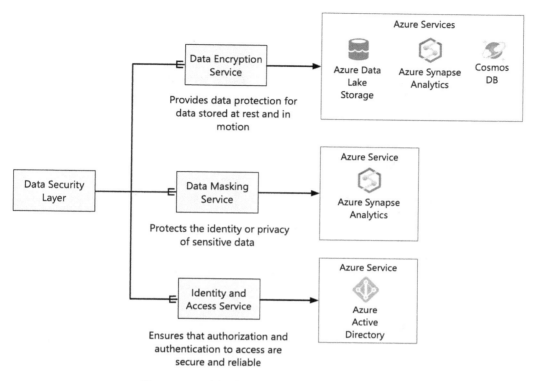

Figure 8.11 – The data security services on Azure

Let's discuss these services in detail.

The first service that we want to discuss is the **Identity and Access Service**:

AD: The AD service is Microsoft's cloud-based identity and access management service. It enables RBAC. It is used to configure access and control for all the Azure resources, including ADLS, Synapse, and Cosmos DB. Azure AD provides a host of services, including self-service password reset, multi-factor authentication, a custom banned password list, and smart lockout features, to name a few.

In addition, it automatically manages identity in Azure Active Directory to authenticate any Azure AD-supported authentication service, including Key Vault. Moreover, Azure AD enables us to gain insights into the security and usage patterns in the Azure environment.

The second service that we want to discuss is the Data Encryption Services, which includes the following:

- **ADLS**: In the data lakehouse architecture, the major components used to store data at rest are the **data lake layer** and the **data serving layer**. As discussed in *Chapter 7, Applying Data Security in a Data Lakehouse*, data encryption is the process of converting data from a readable format into an encoded format. Once encrypted, the data can only be read or processed after it's been decrypted. ADLS uses the encryption provided by the underlying Azure Storage. Azure Storage uses **server-side encryption (SSE)** to automatically encrypt your data when it is persisted in the cloud. By default, data in Azure Storage is encrypted and decrypted using 256-bit **Advanced Encryption Standard (AES)** encryption specification. You can also change the encryption specification to be configured with **customer-managed keys** stored in **Azure Key Vault (AKV)**. Azure Storage also enforces **Transport Level Security (TLS)** while the data is in transit.

- **Azure Synapse Analytics – Transparent Data Encryption (TDE)**: Azure Synapse Analytics provides multiple levels of encryption. As Azure Synapse Analytics uses ADLS for storing data, the first level of encryption is provided by ADLS by default. In addition to this, you can configure Synapse workspaces to have an additional layer of encryption using customer-managed keys. Synapse workspaces support RSA 2048 and 3072 byte-sized keys, as well as RSA-HSM keys. The users can use the customer-managed keys to encrypt SQL pools (dedicated and serverless), Spark pools, and Synapse pipelines. Azure Synapse also provides **Column-Level Encryption (CLE)**, which helps customers implement fine-grained protection of sensitive data within a table.

- **Cosmos DB**: Cosmos DB also encrypts data at rest. Cosmos DB stores its primary databases on **Solid-State Drives (SSDs)**. It uses the exact 256-bit AES encryption specification to encrypt ADLS.

Let's now discuss the service that enables data masking – **Data Masking Service**:

- **Azure Synapse Analytics – dynamic data masking**: Azure Synapse Analytics supports dynamic data masking. This masks sensitive data and thus limits its exposure to non-privileged users. A set policy in the Azure portal based on rules must be configured for the designated fields to be masked. The data is masked using a masking function. The masking functions are a set of methods that control the exposure of data for different scenarios. Some of the masking functions available in Azure Synapse Analytics are as follows:

- **Default**: Full masking masks the entire data according to the data types of the designated fields, that is, using XXXX or fewer Xs if the size of the field is less than four characters for string data types (nchar, ntext, and nvarchar).

- **Credit card**: Credits cards have fixed lengths. The masking method exposes the last four digits of the designated fields and adds a constant string as a prefix.

- **Email**: The masking method for an email exposes the first letter. It replaces the domain with XXX.com, using a constant string prefix in the form of an email address.

Finally, let's now discuss the network security services:

- **Azure Virtual Network (VNET)**: Azure VNET enables the creation of private virtual networks that extend the external network (on-premises or on the cloud) to the Azure cloud. VNET enables the secure communication of Azure resources with the internet or other external networks. Since VNET is cloud-based, it brings additional functionality native to the cloud, that is, scale, availability, and isolation.

- **Azure Firewall**: Azure Firewall is a cloud-native and intelligent network firewall security service. It provides holistic threat protection to the resources in Azure. Being a cloud-native service, it is scalable, highly available, and requires minimal maintenance. In addition, the premium version of the service includes advanced capabilities such as a signature-based **Intrusion detection and prevention systems (IDPS)** that allows rapid detection of attacks by looking for specific patterns. Multiple Azure firewalls can be centrally managed using Azure Firewall Manager. Firewall Manager applies a standard set of network/application rules and configuration to the firewalls and leverages a firewall policy specific to the tenant.

- **Azure VPN Gateway**: As discussed in *Chapter 7, Applying Data Security in a Data Lakehouse*, a VPN gateway is a specific virtual network gateway that sends encrypted traffic between two networks. Azure VPN Gateway establishes secure connectivity between the virtual network within Azure and the external network. Azure VPN Gateway sends the encrypted virtual networks over Microsoft's Azure network.

We have covered services that can be used to implement all the layers of a data lakehouse on Azure. Let's now briefly summarize what we have covered.

Summary

This chapter gave a flavor of how the concept of the data lakehouse is implemented on a cloud computing platform. We started this chapter by delving into the question of *why cloud computing is apt for implementing a data lakehouse*. Then, we revisited the factors that propel cloud computing as the most optimal platform for implementing the data lakehouse architecture. The next section of the chapter focused on implementing the data lakehouse architecture on Microsoft Azure. We peeled back layer after layer and discussed the Azure services that you can use to realize each specific component.

We started with the data ingestion layer and discussed services such as Azure Data Factory and Event Hubs that enable batch and stream data ingestion. Next, we moved on to the data processing layer. We explored services such as Azure Databricks, ADF's data flows, Azure Data Explorer, and HDInsight that can be used to process batch and streaming data. Next, we focused on the data lake layer, where we discussed the Azure Data Lake Storage service. Then, in the fourth layer, the data serving layer, we discussed how services such as Azure Synapse, Cosmos DB, and Azure Data Share enable data serving. The fifth layer that we discussed was the data analytics layer. This layer explored services such as Azure Databricks – SQL, Azure Synapse – serverless pool, Azure Machine Learning, and Power BI that enable analytical sandboxes, machine learning, and business intelligence capabilities. We then discussed the sixth layer, data governance, and how Azure Purview enables data cataloging in the cloud. The final layer that we discussed was the data security layer. This section explored the services that enable identity and access management, data encryption, data masking, and network security in Azure.

In the next chapter, we will extrapolate the concept of the data lakehouse and discuss the macro-architecture patterns of an **enterprise data hub** and an **enterprise data mesh**. We will also discuss a few case studies that exemplify the practical implementation of the data lakehouse.

Further reading

For more information regarding the topics that were covered in this chapter, take a look at the following resources:

- *Azure Data Factory*: `https://azure.microsoft.com/en-us/services/data-factory/`

- *Copy Data Tool*: `https://docs.microsoft.com/en-us/azure/data-factory/quickstart-create-data-factory-copy-data-tool`

- *Synapse Pipelines*: `https://docs.microsoft.com/en-us/azure/synapse-analytics/get-started-pipelines`

- *Event Hub*: https://azure.microsoft.com/en-us/services/event-hubs/

- *IoT Hub*: https://azure.microsoft.com/en-gb/services/iot-hub/

- *Apache Kafka*: https://kafka.apache.org/

- *HDInsight*: https://azure.microsoft.com/en-us/services/hdinsight/

- *Apache Kafka Introduction*: https://docs.microsoft.com/en-us/azure/hdinsight/kafka/apache-kafka-introduction

- *Azure Data Lake Storage*: https://azure.microsoft.com/en-us/services/storage/data-lake-storage/

- *Azure Databricks*: https://docs.microsoft.com/en-us/azure/databricks/scenarios/what-is-azure-databricks

- *Spark Structured Streaming*: https://spark.apache.org/docs/latest/structured-streaming-programming-guide.html

- *Spark Concepts*: https://docs.microsoft.com/en-us/azure/synapse-analytics/spark/apache-spark-concepts

- *Azure Stream Analytics*: https://azure.microsoft.com/en-gb/services/stream-analytics/

- *Azure Stream Analytics*: https://docs.microsoft.com/en-gb/azure/stream-analytics/stream-analytics-introduction

- *Data Explorer*: https://azure.microsoft.com/en-us/services/data-explorer/

- *Kusto Query Language*: https://docs.microsoft.com/en-us/azure/data-explorer/kusto/query/

- *Apache Spark*: https://docs.microsoft.com/en-us/azure/hdinsight/spark/apache-spark-overview

- *Apache Spark*: https://spark.apache.org/

- *Azure Synapse Analytics*: https://docs.microsoft.com/en-us/azure/synapse-analytics/sql-data-warehouse/sql-data-warehouse-overview-what-is?context=/azure/synapse-analytics/context/context

- *Massively Parallel Processing*: https://docs.microsoft.com/en-us/azure/synapse-analytics/sql-data-warehouse/massively-parallel-processing-mpp-architecture

- *Cosmos DB*: `https://azure.microsoft.com/en-us/services/cosmos-db/`

- *Cosmos DB*: `https://docs.microsoft.com/en-us/rest/api/cosmos-db/`

- *On-Demand Cluster*: `https://docs.microsoft.com/en-us/azure/synapse-analytics/sql/on-demand-workspace-overview`

- *Power BI Overview*: `https://docs.microsoft.com/en-us/power-bi/fundamentals/power-bi-overview`

- *Power BI Security*: `https://powerbi.microsoft.com/en-us/security/`

- *Power BI Security*: `https://docs.microsoft.com/en-us/power-bi/admin/service-admin-power-bi-security`

- *Storage Encryption*: `https://docs.microsoft.com/en-us/azure/storage/common/storage-service-encryption`

- *Advanced Encryption Standard*: `https://en.wikipedia.org/wiki/Advanced_Encryption_Standard`

- *Synapse Encryption*: `https://docs.microsoft.com/en-us/azure/synapse-analytics/security/workspaces-encryption`

- *Column-level Encryption*: `https://azure.microsoft.com/en-us/updates/columnlevel-encryption-for-azure-synapse-analytics/`

- *Dynamic Data Masking*: `https://docs.microsoft.com/en-us/azure/azure-sql/database/dynamic-data-masking-overview`

- *Azure Active Directory*: `https://docs.microsoft.com/en-us/azure/active-directory/fundamentals/active-directory-whatis`

- *Azure Virtual Network*: `https://docs.microsoft.com/en-us/azure/virtual-network/virtual-networks-overview`

- *Azure Firewall*: `https://docs.microsoft.com/en-us/azure/firewall/overview`

- *VPN Gateways*: `https://docs.microsoft.com/en-us/azure/vpn-gateway/vpn-gateway-about-vpngateways`

9
Scaling the Data Lakehouse Architecture

In the journey so far, we have covered all the seven layers of the data lakehouse architecture. However, for large organizations that are complex and spread globally, a single data lakehouse won't suffice. They will need multiple platforms to fulfill their analytical requirements. In addition, they will need a structured process to share data elements between them. Therefore, the need arises to develop a **macro-architecture** pattern that ensures that the organization's overall analytical requirements are met without compromising the architectural debts.

This chapter will discuss concepts that you can use to develop those macro-architecture patterns. First, we will define the need for a macro-architecture pattern for a data lakehouse and the organizational drivers that dictate the requirements for such a pattern. Next, we will cover two types of macro-architecture patterns, namely **hub-spoke** and **data mesh**. This section will discuss the concept, the typical conceptual architecture for these **macro patterns**, and how the idea of the data lakehouse interlaces with these patterns.

In summary, we will cover the following in this chapter:

- The need for a macro-architectural pattern for analytics
- Implementing a data lakehouse in the macro-architectural pattern

Let's begin by discussing the need for macro patterns for large organizations.

The need for a macro-architectural pattern for analytics

Organizations are complex and need to evolve in their analytics journey, especially when they become too big to be managed centrally. Typically, a complex organization has two groups, the central unit and the sub-units.

- **Central unit**: This is the unit that is at the organizational level. It may prescribe guidances that are expected to be followed by the sub-units. It may hold budgets that are distributed for various initiatives across the sub-units. It may also have platforms that fulfill group-level requirements.

- **Sub-units**: It is not uncommon for organizations to have many sub-units. The sub-units may have differing levels of independence from the central unit. This degree of autonomy is based on the organizational structure and its culture. Typically, these sub-units can belong to mainly three categories:

  - The first category comprises a different organization (entity) within a group organization in the same or another geography.

  - The second category comprises an independent business unit within the same organization.

  - The third category is an intra-organizational department.

Each of these sub-units may have its analytics journey. As a result, a single data lakehouse won't be able to fulfill the multitudes of requirements that each of these sub-units may have. Five key considerations that mandate a different analytics journey for any sub-units are as follows:

- **The uniqueness of requirements**: The requirements that can be fulfilled at the central level may not be sufficient at the sub-unit level. The sub-units will have their needs based on their markets or regulations. Therefore, it will not be feasible for the central unit to cater to all the requirements of the sub-units.

- **Current skill sets**: The technical or functional skills available at the central unit may not suffice to fulfill the evolving requirements of the sub-units. These may demand specialized skills such as those in marketing or supply chain. These specialized skills are attuned to the needs of the sub-units.

- **Regulatory compliance**: There are a lot of regulatory and compliance rules that need to be followed, especially in highly regulated industries such as banking and healthcare. The data is mandated to be in-country. Hence, the in-country organization needs to have an analytics platform for supporting local requirements. This requirement will call for the decoupling of central units from the sub-units.

- **Budgetary constraints**: Based on how organizations are structured, the budgets for analytics programs may be controlled centrally or by sub-units. Based on these budget controls, the sub-units will be independent of decoupling themselves from the central unit and pursuing their analytical journey.

- **Cultural aspects**: Last but not least, the culture of an organization plays a critical role in how directions from the central units are perceived, accepted, and implemented by the sub-units. Culture is unique in an organization's DNA. It has nuances that can't be dealt with by technology. However, this dimension can't be ignored when framing the macro-architecture pattern for analytics.

These five factors justify the need for a macro-architectural pattern for analytics that organizations can adopt to scale their analytics ambitions and be more data-driven. There are two types of macro-architectural patterns that we will discuss. The first one is the hub-spoke pattern, and the second one is the data mesh pattern. Both these patterns have some similarities in their approach of implementation along with differences. Let's discuss each of these patterns in detail.

Now that the need for a macro-architectural pattern for analytics has been established, let's discuss how these patterns are implemented with a data lakehouse.

Implementing a data lakehouse in a macro-architectural pattern

The building block for both these patterns is a **node**. The following figure depicts the formation of a node:

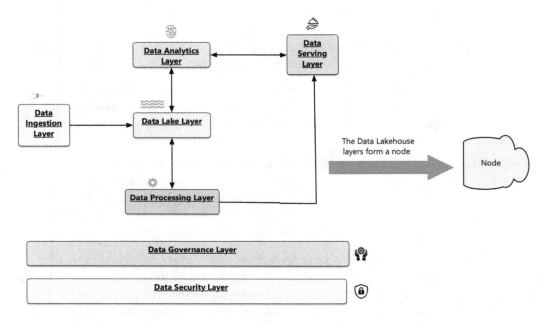

Figure 9.1 – A node – the building block for the macro-architecture pattern

A node is the data lakehouse architectural component implemented in the organization's sub-units and the central unit. The hub-spoke and the data mesh patterns differ in how the data is discovered and shared between the nodes. Let's discuss these patterns in detail.

The hub-spoke pattern

The first pattern that we want to discuss is the hub-spoke pattern. The following figure depicts the conceptual architecture of the hub-spoke pattern:

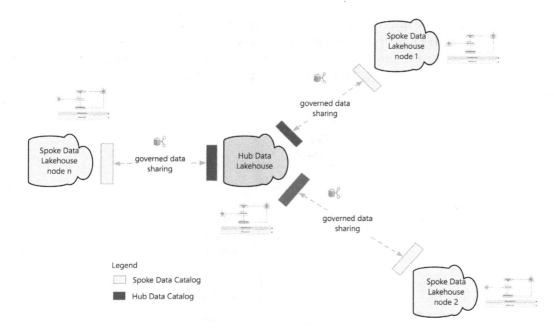

Figure 9.2 – The conceptual architecture of the hub-spoke pattern

A central node acts as a hub in the hub-spoke pattern, and many edge nodes act as the spoke. The hub is the central node that orchestrates and governs the data sharing between each of the spokes. Each spoke node can have its own data lakehouse. The way the spoke nodes are constructed depends on the organizational structure. It can be at a department level, a separate organizational unit, or even a sub-department within a large department.

The data lakehouse of both a hub and spokes are cataloged. Cataloging will ensure that the metadata of the data elements in each of the data lakehouses are available for browsing and exploring.

A governed data sharing layer facilitates data sharing between the hub node and the spoke node. For instance, in a hub-spoke architecture, data is only shared between the hub and the spoke and not between the spoke nodes. An organization may have more steps in the data-sharing process. However, the workflow depicted in the following figure should suffice for most organizations:

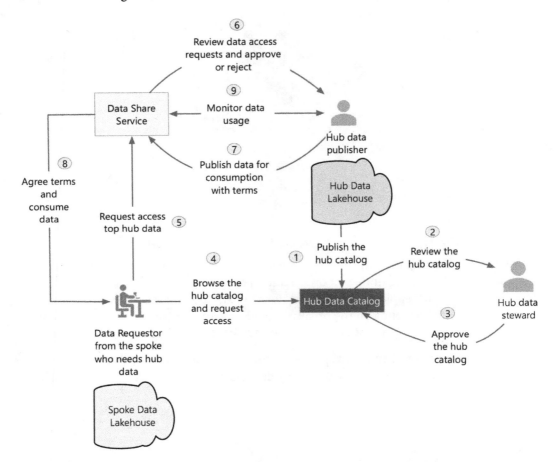

Figure 9.3 – The hub to spoke data sharing workflow

In this scenario, **Spoke Data Lakehouse** has a data requestor who requests data from the hub. But, first, let's go through the workflow steps in detail:

1. Firstly, the data publishers, who have the data ownership, publish the metadata of the data lakehouse node into the data catalog.

2. The hub node steward reviews the published catalog to ensure that it is aligned to the governance framework of the hub node.

3. The steward then approves or rejects the published catalog contents. If approved, the catalog is updated with the metadata.

4. When a spoke data requestor requires data from the hub node, the data requestor browses the hub data catalog to identify the data of interest.

5. Once the data of interest is identified, the data requestor requests the data from the hub through **Data Share Service**.

6. The request for data access is routed to the data publisher. The data publisher reviews the request and approves or rejects the request for data access.

7. If the request is approved, the data publisher shares the data with the data requestor through **Data Share Service**, which enables data sharing between the hub and the spoke nodes. The terms of data usage are also clarified.

8. Finally, the data requestor reviews the terms of data usage. Upon the acceptance of the terms, the data requestor can start consuming the data usage.

9. The data publisher constantly monitors the data usage pattern through **Data Share Service**.

The following figure depicts another scenario where the task is reversed. In this scenario, a hub data requestor requests data from the spoke node. The workflow is similar to the steps placed in the previous list. However, the roles of the requestor and publisher are reversed:

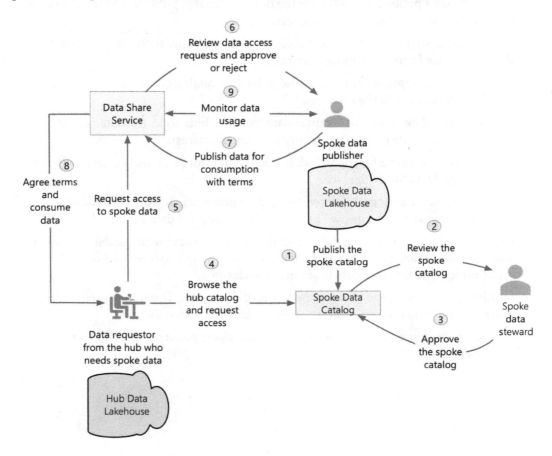

Figure 9.4 – The spoke to hub data sharing workflow

We have covered the concept of the hub-spoke architecture and the workflow for data sharing between the hub and spoke. Let's now dive deep into the idea of data mesh and the workflow associated with it.

The data mesh pattern

The second pattern that we want to discuss is the data mesh pattern. *Thoughtworks*, a global technology company, introduced the concept of data mesh as a new paradigm that takes inspiration from modern distributed architecture and treats data as a product. It strives for the convergence of **distributed domain-driven architecture**, **self-serve platform design**, and **product thinking** with data. The conceptual underpinning of the data mesh architecture can be abstracted and applied in a distributed and scalable data lakehouse architecture pattern.

The following figure depicts the conceptual architecture of a data mesh pattern when applied to the data lakehouse:

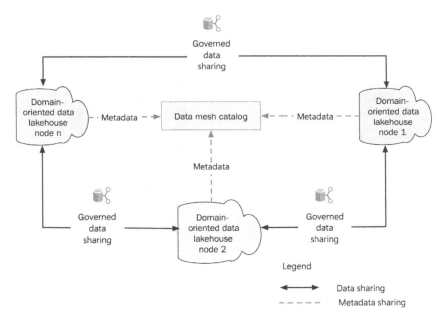

Figure 9.5 – The conceptual architecture of data mesh

The data mesh pattern doesn't feature a central node and is *loosely coupled* compared to a hub-spoke architecture. It has different data lakehouse nodes that are independent of each other. The node data lakehouses are **domain-driven**. A **domain** can be oriented in multiple ways. The original idea of data mesh alludes to a source-oriented domain aligning to business processes. However, a more practical approach would be to define a domain based on the organizational setup and practicality; for example, a domain can be a **product group**, it can be separate organizational entities, and it can also be a specific business process, such as marketing. Each domain has its own data lakehouse that is managed and maintained by that domain.

Each domain data lakehouse may opt to have its data catalog. However, the critical component in this architecture is the **data mesh catalog**. The data mesh catalog is the master catalog used to discover the data elements available in different nodes. Each domain-oriented node will donate its metadata to the data mesh catalog. This donation of metadata determines the effectiveness of the data mesh architecture. Once the metadata is contributed, other nodes can browse through the data mesh catalog. They can select the data of interest and mutually share data between the nodes through a governed data sharing process. The critical point to note here is that, unlike the hub-spoke architecture, the data mesh architecture enables data sharing between the "spoke nodes." There is no hub node in a data mesh architecture. Instead, each node of the data mesh has a Data Share service that enables seamless data sharing:

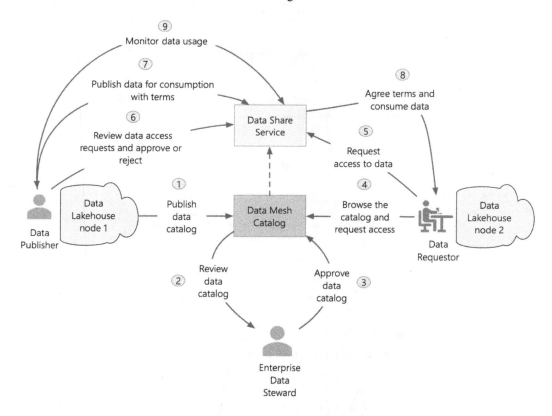

Figure 9.6 – The data sharing workflow in data mesh

The preceding figure illustrates the workflow for a scenario of data sharing between two nodes in a data mesh architecture:

1. Firstly, the data publishers, who have the data ownership, publish the metadata of the data lakehouse node into the data catalog.

2. The enterprise data mesh steward reviews the published catalog to ensure that it is aligned to the organization's governance framework.

3. The steward then approves or rejects the published catalog contents. If approved, the catalog is updated with the metadata.

4. When a data requestor from one node requires the data from another node, the data requestor browses the data mesh catalog to identify the data of interest.

5. Once the data of interest is identified, the data requestor requests the data from the hub through the Data Share service.

6. The request for data access is routed to the data publisher. The data publisher reviews the request and approves or rejects the request for data access.

7. If the request is approved, the data publisher shares the data with the data requestor through the Data Share service, which enables data sharing between the nodes. As in the hub-spoke architecture, the terms of data usage are also clarified.

8. Finally, the data requestor reviews the terms of data usage. Upon the acceptance of the terms, the data requestor can start consuming the data usage.

9. The data publisher constantly monitors the data usage pattern through the Data Share service.

We have covered the concepts of hub-spoke and data mesh architecture. Let's now discuss the framework that you can use to choose between a hub-spoke and a data mesh architecture.

Choosing between hub-spoke and data mesh

Whether an organization adopts a hub-spoke pattern or a data mesh pattern depends on many factors. Factors such as organizational maturity, internal culture, data landscape, and analytics maturity influence the right choice of pattern. These factors are unique to an organization. However, *two* key drivers are consistent across organizations:

1. **The ability to share data**: The first driver is the extent to which the data landscape needs to be shared within all the sub-units and the central unit of the organization. Ideally, for complete data sharing, every sub-unit needs to have a comprehensive view of what data is available with the central unit and other sub-units. However, this may not be the case every time. For example, there can be scenarios where sub-units are bounded by regulatory or legal constraints, especially in highly regulated industries. This constraint would imply that you can share selective data between the sub-units and the central units.

2. **The degree of independence between the sub-units**: The second driver is the extent to which the sub-units are independent concerning the central unit and other sub-units. At one end of the spectrum, the sub-units are separate entities and run as independent organizations. They have low or no dependency on the central units or other sub-units. In this scenario, the degree of independence is higher. At the other end of the spectrum, the sub-unit is dependent on the central unit or other sub-units for its day-to-day functioning. In this case, the degree of independence is lower. In practice, every sub-unit will be somewhere in the middle of the spectrum. They are independent in many aspects of their day-to-day work. Still, they are dependent on other sub-units or the central units for some aspects of their functioning.

The following figure depicts a potential selection criterion between hub-spoke and data mesh:

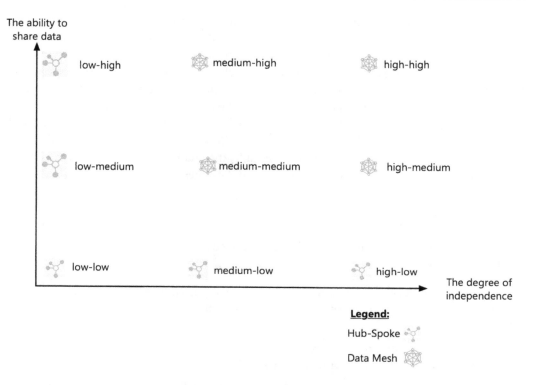

Figure 9.7 – A potential selection criterion between hub-spoke and data mesh

From the preceding figure, you can gauge that a data mesh architecture is recommended where there is a higher degree of independence between the sub-units and a higher ability to share data. Conversely, a hub-spoke architecture is recommended when the level of autonomy for the sub-units is lower.

Let's now summarize what we have covered in this chapter.

Summary

Large organizations evolve and their analytics journeys differ. A single data lakehouse will not be able to cater to all the analytical requirements of the organization. Therefore, the data lakehouse architecture needs to be scaled in a governed manner to address the ever-changing analytical requirements. In addition, the data in the data lakehouse needs to be democratized and enable structured data sharing between the different units of the organization. This chapter covered the methods for scaling the data lakehouse architecture pattern.

The chapter started by emphasizing the need for macro patterns. We defined the two categories of units that embody a large organization and the five key considerations that influence the analytical requirements of these units. The next section of the chapter focused on implementing the two general macro-architecture patterns. The hub-spoke pattern was the first pattern that we discussed. The section covered the key components that develop this architecture and how data is shared between the hub and spoke components. The data mesh pattern was the second pattern that we discussed. We covered the key components that develop the data mesh architecture and how data is shared between different components of data mesh. Finally, the chapter discussed a framework that you can use to choose between hub-spoke and data mesh.

Further reading

For more information regarding the topics that were covered in this chapter, take a look at the following resources:

- *How to Move Beyond a Monolithic Data Lake to a Distributed Data Mesh*: `https://martinfowler.com/articles/data-monolith-to-mesh.html`

- *What is Data Mesh (Staburst)*: `https://www.starburst.io/learn/data-fundamentals/what-is-data-mesh/`

- *Domain data as a product*: `https://martinfowler.com/articles/data-monolith-to-mesh.html#DomainDataAsAProduct`

Index

Graphics Interchange Format (GIF) 69
graphics processing units (GPU) 95
grouping-based actions
  types 55

H

Hadoop
  about 12
  divide and conquer 13
hash distribution 151
HBase 78
HDInsight (HDI) 145
holistic IAM strategy
  elements 122
horizontal scaling (scale-out) 50
hub-spoke network topology 130
hub-spoke pattern
  about 166
  architecture 167
  data sharing workflow 169
  versus data mesh pattern 174
human-readable format (plaintext) 125
Hypertext Transfer Protocol
  Secure (HTTPS) 126

I

IAM component
  capabilities 123, 124
Identity and Access Management (IAM)
  about 121
  two-step process 123
  using, in data lakehouse 121-124
intermediate datastore 65
International Data Corporation (IDC) 8
Internet of Things (IoT) 8, 22, 78
Internet of Things (IoT) Hub 144

J

Java Database Connectivity (JDBC) 48
JavaScript Object Notation
  (JSON) format 21, 69
Joint Photographic Experts
  Group (JPEG) 69
Jupyter Notebook 85

K

key-value stores 77
Kusto Query Language (KQL) 148

L

Lambda architecture pattern
  about 56, 57
  batch layer 57
  serving layer 58
  speed layer 58
logical architecture
  about 141
  requirements 25
logical data lakehouse architecture
  developing 25, 26
logical data model 110

M

machine learning 86
machine learning, categories
  supervised learning 87
  unsupervised learning 88
machine learning model
  life cycle stages 88

`Packt.com`

Subscribe to our online digital library for full access to over 7,000 books and videos, as well as industry leading tools to help you plan your personal development and advance your career. For more information, please visit our website.

Why subscribe?

- Spend less time learning and more time coding with practical eBooks and Videos from over 4,000 industry professionals
- Improve your learning with Skill Plans built especially for you
- Get a free eBook or video every month
- Fully searchable for easy access to vital information
- Copy and paste, print, and bookmark content

Did you know that Packt offers eBook versions of every book published, with PDF and ePub files available? You can upgrade to the eBook version at `packt.com` and as a print book customer, you are entitled to a discount on the eBook copy. Get in touch with us at `customercare@packtpub.com` for more details.

At `www.packt.com`, you can also read a collection of free technical articles, sign up f or a range of free newsletters, and receive exclusive discounts and offers on Packt books and eBooks.

Other Books You May Enjoy

If you enjoyed this book, you may be interested in these other books by Packt:

Limitless Analytics with Azure Synapse

ISBN: 9781800205659

- Explore the necessary considerations for data ingestion and orchestration while building analytical pipelines
- Understand pipelines and activities in Synapse pipelines and use them to construct end-to-end data-driven workflows
- Query data using various coding languages on Azure Synapse
- Focus on Synapse SQL and Synapse Spark
- Manage and monitor resource utilization and query activity in Azure Synapse
- Connect Power BI workspaces with Azure Synapse and create or modify reports directly from Synapse Studio
- Create and manage IP firewall rules in Azure Synapse

Data Engineering with Apache Spark, Delta Lake, and Lakehouse

ISBN: 9781801077743

- Discover the challenges you may face in the data engineering world
- Add ACID transactions to Apache Spark using Delta Lake
- Understand effective design strategies to build enterprise-grade data lakes
- Explore architectural and design patterns for building efficient data ingestion pipelines
- Orchestrate a data pipeline for preprocessing data using Apache Spark and Delta Lake APIs
- Automate deployment and monitoring of data pipelines in production
  Get to grips with securing, monitoring, and managing data pipelines models efficiently

Packt is searching for authors like you

If you're interested in becoming an author for Packt, please visit `authors.`
`packtpub.com` and apply today. We have worked with thousands of developers and
tech professionals, just like you, to help them share their insight with the global tech
community. You can make a general application, apply for a specific hot topic that we are
recruiting an author for, or submit your own idea.

Share your thoughts

Now you've finished *Data Lakehouse in Action*, we'd love to hear your thoughts! Scan the
QR code below to go straight to the Amazon review page for this book and share your
feedback or leave a review on the site that you purchased it from.

https://packt.link/r/1-801-81593-3

Your review is important to us and the tech community and will help us make sure we're
delivering excellent quality content.